1939-1945

WORLD WAR TWO

AUTHOR

Francesco Mattesini, born in Arezzo on 14 April 1936, resident in Rome since the summer of 1951, he served between February 1958 and July 1999 in the IV Department of the Army General Staff. A scholar and expert on air-sea warfare, a skilful and meticulous researcher, he was an active contributor to the Giornale d'Italia for which he edited the "Verità Storiche" column. He has written, revealing many behind-the-scenes stories, numerous political-military articles in newspapers and the specialised press, and published, in the 1980s, with private publishers, the volumes "La battaglia d'Inghilterra"; "Il giallo di Matapan"; "La battaglia aeronavale di mezzo agosto"; and with co-author, but only for the political part, Prof. Alberto Santoni, "La partecipazione tedesca alla guerra aeronavale nel Mediterraneo", in its second edition, (2005), of which he edited the entire research, operational, statistical and graphic part. A collaborator of the Ufficio Storico della Marina Militare, from which he was commissioned to carry out a strict and precise historical review of the books published in the years 1950-1980, Mattesini published "La battaglia di Punta Stilo"; "Betasom. La guerra negli Oceani" (The War in the Oceans); "La battaglia di Capo Teulada" (The Battle of Cape Teulada); "L'Operazione Gaudo e lo scontro notturno di Capo Matapan" (Operation Gaudo and the Night Battle of Cape Matapan); "La Marina e l'8 Settembre" (The Navy and September 8), in two volumes; and the first four volumes of the series "Correspondence and Technical-Operational Directives of Supermarina" (1939-1941), as well as 60 essays for the Bollettino d'Archivio dell'Ufficio Storico della Marina Militare (Navy History Office Archive Bulletin). At the same time, for the Air Force Historical Office, Mattesini produced the two-volume series (four tomes), 'The technical-operational directives of Superaereo 1940-1943', and the volume 'Italian-German air activity in the Mediterranean, January-May 1941'. In 2019-2020, Mattesini published 'Lights and Shadows of Italian Aircraft August 1940 - September 1943'; 'The Mid-August Airship Battle' revised and updated; 'Punta Stilo 9 July 1940, 80th anniversary of the first airship battle in history'; 'The Ambush of Matapan'; 'The Mid-June Airship Battle'; 'The Yellow of Cape Bon'; 8 September 1943'. "From the Armistice to the Myth of the Defence of Porta San Paolo"; "The Blockade of Malta and the "C.3". He has been a member for many years of the Society of Military History (SISM) and the Italian Association of Naval Maritime Documentation (AIDMEN), for which he has produced several essays, and many others on his Academia Edu site page. For Luca Cristini publisher to date he has almost a dozen titles to his credit, including in the History series: 'La notte di Taranto dell'11 novembre 1941', 'La battaglia di Creta maggio 1941, La guerra civile spagnola e la Regia Marina italiana, Testimonianze di guerra nell'estate del 1944 a Castel Focognano e L'attacco dei sommergibili tedeschi e italiani nei mari delle Indie occidentali (1942) and many others.

PUBLISHING'S NOTES

None of unpublished images or text of our book may be reproduced in any format without the expressed written permission of Luca Cristini Editore (already Soldiershop.com) when not indicate as marked with license creative commons 3.0 or 4.0. Luca Cristini Editore has made every reasonable effort to locate, contact and acknowledge rights holders and to correctly apply terms and conditions to Content. Every effort has been made to trace the copyright of all the photographs. If there are unintentional omissions, please contact the publisher in writing at: info@soldiershop.com, who will correct all subsequent editions.

Our trademark: Luca Cristini Editore©, and the names of our series & brand: Soldiershop, Witness to war, Museum book, Bookmoon, Soldiers&Weapons, Battlefield, War in colour, Historical Biographies, Darwin's view, Fabula, Altrastoria, Italia Storica Ebook, Witness To History, Soldiers, Weapons & Uniforms, Storia etc. are herein © by Luca Cristini Editore.

LICENSES COMMONS

This book may utilize part of material marked with license creative commons 3.0 or 4.0 (CC BY 4.0), (CC BY-ND 4.0), (CC BY-SA 4.0) or (CC0 1.0). We give appropriate attribution credit and indicate if change were made in the acknowledgments field. Our WTW books series utilize only fonts licensed under the SIL Open Font License or other free use license.

For a complete list of Soldiershop titles please contact Luca Cristini Editore on our website: www.soldiershop.com or www.cristinieditore.com. E-mail: info@soldiershop.com

To the memory of Giulio Bonetti known as Bepi, who perished in the waters of the Tunisian Sea, and Vittorio Cividini, also present at the battle, both from Zanica (BG).

Title: **THE NAVAL BATTLE OF 2 DECEMBER 1942 IN THE SICILY CHANNEL** Code.: **WTW-050** EN
By Francesco Mattesini.
ISBN code: 9791255890270 First edition October 2023
Language: English, Size:177,8x254mm Cover & Art Design: Luca S. Cristini

WITNESS TO WAR (SOLDIERSHOP) is a trademark of Luca Cristini Editore, via Orio, 35/4 - 24050 Zanica (BG) ITALY.

WITNESS TO WAR

THE NAVAL BATTLE OF 2 DECEMBER 1942 IN THE SICILY CHANNEL

THE ATTACK BY THE BRITISH 'Q FORCE', WITH THE DESTRUCTION OF THE ITALIAN CONVOY 'AVENTINO' AND THE EMBARRASSING MISTAKE OF THE DESTROYER CAMICIA NERA

PHOTOS & IMAGES FROM WORLD WARTIME ARCHIVES

FRANCESCO MATTESINI

BOOKS TO COLLECT

CONTENTS

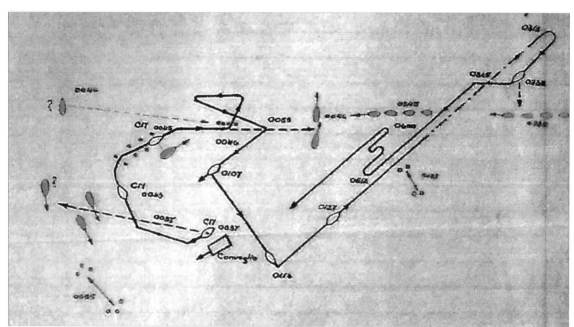

▲ The battle of the convoy 'Aventino' according to the map attached to the *Camicia Nera* Destroyer Report. In black the Italian ships and the route of the Camicia Nera, in solid grey what the movements of the British ships looked like.

THE MOVEMENTS OF ITALIAN CONVOYS TO TUNISIA

The Battle of Banco Skerki, which occurred north of Bizerte at around 01.00 a.m. on 2 December 1942 (Wednesday), was the most important and also the bloodiest, in terms of the naval and human losses suffered by the Italian navy, of all those fought for the defence of Italian-German traffic in the first six months of the campaign for the possession of Tunisia, which began on 8 November 1942 with the Allied landings at Casablanca, Oran and Algiers and ended with the surrender of the Axis forces on the Cape Bon Peninsula on 11 May 1943.

The need to bring an increasing amount of supplies to the fighting troops in Tunisia led, towards the end of November, to the organisation of four convoys (called B, C, G and H) in Italian ports, which were simultaneously at sea on the night of 1 to 2 December, bound for Bizerte, Tunis and Tripoli.

Convoy B, which left Naples at 14:30 on 30 November, consisted of the steamers *Arlesiana*, *Achille Lauro*, *Campania*, *Menes* and *Lisboa*, the latter two German, while the escort included the torpedo boats *Sirius* (command ship), *Groppo*, *Orione* and *Pallade*. At 07:10 on 1 December, following the news that enemy naval units were at Bona, the convoy B's escort, whose speed was only 7 knots, was reinforced by the torpedo boat *Uragano* from Trapani, and later, at 19:35, it was joined by the destroyers *Maestrale*, *Ascari* and *Grecale, the* only ones available at the time, which had laid a barrage of mines in the Sicilian Channel during the night. The order, issued at 15.08, was motivated *'against the possible coming from Bona where a few destroyers were present this morning'*. [1]

Convoy C, which also departed from Naples bound for Tripoli at 11pm on 30 November, consisted of the steamers *Chisone*, *Veloce* and *Devoli*, and an escort consisting of the torpedo boats *Lupo* (command ship), *Aretusa*, *Sagittario* and *Ardente*.

Convoy G, which left Palermo for Tunis at 09.00 on 1 December, comprised the sole tanker *Giorgio* escorted by the destroyer *Lampo* (command ship) and the torpedo boat *Climene*.

Finally, convoy H, which set sail from Palermo for Bizerte at 10.00 am on 1 December, comprised the three merchant ships *Aventino*, *Puccini*, *K.T. 1* (German motor vessel *Kappa Tau 1*), which were joined at 5.30 pm by the ferry *Aspromonte, which* left Trapani at 3.30 pm. The escort consisted of the destroyers *Da Recco* (command ship), *Camicia Nera*, *Folgore* and the *torpedo* boats *Procione* and *Clio*. [2]

A total of thirteen merchant ships and nineteen escorts were on the move in the convoys: seven destroyers and twelve torpedo boats. To these ships were added two more torpedo boats, the *Partenope* and the *Perseo*, which were destined to proceed the convoys

---

1   AUSMM, *Departure Message* of 1 December 1942-XXI, with telegraph protocol no. 539155.

2   Convoy H carried 1,177 soldiers (half on the *Aventino* and half on the *Puccini*), 689 tons of war material, including 120 tons of ammunition, 12 cannons with their equipment, 32 trucks and 4 tanks, all on K.T. 1.

on the route to Tunisia in order to carry out, with the echogoniometers (the corresponding acoustic underwater search apparatus of the British asdic and the US sonar) in operation, an anti-submarine rake, but at the same time to detect the presence of enemy surface ships so that the convoys could avoid a possible *'night-time encounter'* by hijacking.[3]

Initially, the movement of the convoys was to begin on 29 November, but it was postponed by Supermarina, the Operational Command of the Regia Marina General Staff, by twenty-four hours. It was also decided that convoys G and H, which left Palermo at 10.00 a.m. on the 30th, and sailing at a speed of 10 knots, should proceed together until midnight and then split up and continue with parallel routes (convoy G further north than convoy H) on the direct route to their respective destinations in Tunisia, the ports of Tunis and Bizerte. [4]

It has been pointed out that Supermarina could have sent the destroyers *Maestrale* (Lieutenant Commander Nicola Bedeschi), *Ascari* and *Grecale*, returning from the laying of mines near the Isola dei Cani (broken S. 96), to reinforce the convoy H escort. But it did not do so in order to assign those three units to the protection of convoy B, which had departed from Naples, and which was considered the most important, and which was commanded on the torpedo boat *Sirius* by Lieutenant Commander Nicola Romualdo Bertone. A memorandum from Supermarina specifies that it was preferred to assign the three destroyers to convoy B, since the convoy "*Aventino*" being "*faster, better protected and in an advanced position, would have found itself, already at midnight on the 1*[st]*, somewhat protected by the shallow waters of the Keith bank*" (6 miles north of the Skerki bank, north of Bizerte, and about 30 miles long with a north-east-southwest orientation), and by the mines of the barrages already placed in that area.[5]

From the interception of the R. Marina radio stations, it appeared that between 14.40 and 20.15 on 1 December, all four convoys had been sighted by British scouts. This, as we shall see, led to the departure of British naval units from Bona and Malta with the intention of intercepting the convoys and destroying them during the night.

All scouts' discovery signals, at the same time intercepted and deciphered also by the listening stations of the Regia Aeronautica and those of the OBS (the German Armed Forces Command of the Southern Front, under the orders of Field Marshal Albert Kesselring, who was also commander of the 2nd Air Fleet - Luftflotte 2.), were relayed back to the air by Supermarina, so that the convoys at sea would be informed and increase their vigilance. The first signal that was intercepted was the discovery, southwest of Naples of the two convoys B and C, reported by an RAF scout at 23.00 on 30 November. The two convoys, sailing in the Tyrrhenian Sea, were reported again the next day, 1 December, at 14.40 and 15.00, and a quarter of an hour later it was the turn of convoy G, departing from Palermo, to be discovered. Then at 8.15 p.m., there was a new air signal interception, this time of convoy H, also departing from Palermo.

---

3 AUSMM, *Supermarina Messaggi in Partenza* No. 1823 directed to the torpedo boat *Partenope*.
4 AUSMM, *Supermarine Departure Messages* No. 98465 of 27 November 1942 and No. 12499 of 29 November 1942.
5 AUSMM, *Composition Convoy 'Aventino'*, 2 December 1942.

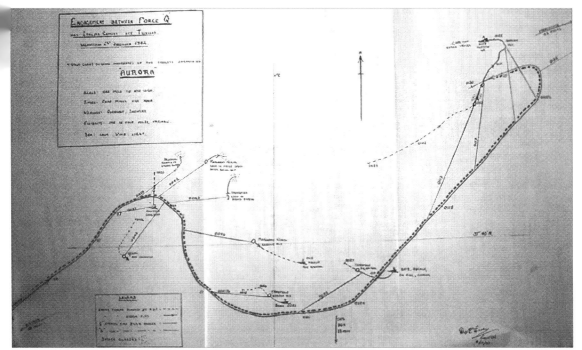

▲ Details of the manoeuvre of the Q Force ships' attack on the 'Aventino' convoy. In the mixed integer and dashes the course of the cruiser Aurora.

All these reports of convoy movements could not fail to alarm Supermarina, not least because it was suspected that enemy ships were intent on intercepting them, particularly those that might arrive from the west. In fact, on the afternoon of 30 November, at 13.30, six unspecified warships had been sighted in the port of Bona, but believed to be a cruiser and five destroyers, and Supermarina calculated that from Bona they could intercept convoys B and H in six hours. A request was then made (through the R. Marina Liaison Office at the OBS, at Villa Falconieri in Frascati, commanded by frigate captain Virginio Rusca) for an aerial reconnaissance over the port of Bona around sunset on 1 December, to ascertain what kind of ships were there.

Asked repeatedly by the OBS about the outcome of that reconnaissance, at 20.35 the news arrived, by telephone, to Superaereo (the Operational Command of the Regia Aeronautica General Staff) that, from the reconnaissance carried out by the German Ju.88D aircraft from the 2nd Squadron of the 122nd Strategic Reconnaissance Group (2.(F)/122) up to 18.00 hours, no movement of enemy ships had been detected at sea, while there was no news of the two aircraft (one German Ju.88 of the 2.(F)/122 and the other Italian, a Cant. Z. 1007 bis of the 51st Strategic Reconnaissance Group) in charge of the mission over Bona. Both had in fact been shot down, Cant Z. 1007 bis at 08.00 by two Spitfires of the RAF's 242nd Squadron, piloted by Lieutenant Thomas Hodgson and Sergeant Like Mallison; it was probably the latter that shot down the Ju. 88.

But on that day, 1 December, something even worse happened, because in order to undermine the British ships in the port of Bona, the Sardinian Air Force sent two formations of offensive aircraft on the attack, in the afternoon, around 3 p.m.; the first consisted

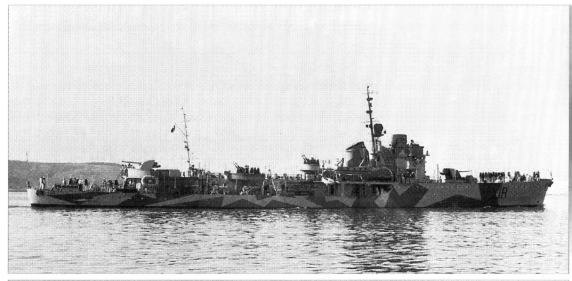

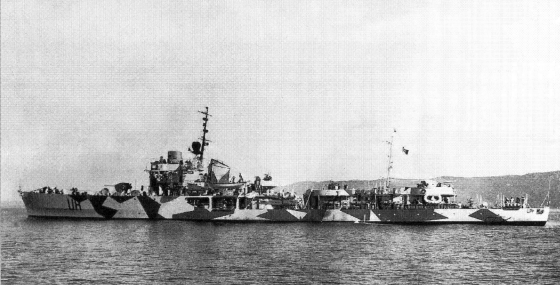

▲ Above: pictured on both sides, the new escort torpedo boat *Uragano*, which went to reinforce the protection to convoy B. The images are from 1942.

▼ The Italian CT *Maestrale* on a war mission.

▲ Villa Falconieri, in Frascati (Rome), where Field Marshal Albert Kesselring exercised his command as Superior Commander of the South (OBS).

▼ In the search for Axis convoys and naval units, the fast US-built Martin A 30 aircraft were used, which in the RAF were known as Baltimore aircraft. Particularly active were the Baltimore aircraft of the 69th Squadron based at the Maltese Luqa airfield.

▲ German Ju.88D aircraft of the 122ⁿᵈ Strategic Reconnaissance Group (F)/122).

▼ Regia Aeronautica Savoia Marchetti S 84 bomber. In the raid on the port of Bona on 1 December 1943, in which ten S.84s took part, three were shot down and three others damaged in the attack by Royal Air Force (RAF) Spitfire V fighter aircraft.

of five Reggiane Re. 2001 of the 22nd Group, armed with 250-kilo bombs which, under the command of Captain Germano La Ferla, carried out a dive-bombing without being able to detect the outcome due to the coverage of the 10/10 target because of the cloud banks; the second action, of little effect, was carried out by ten Savoia Marchetti S. 84 of the 32nd Wing; three (piloted by the commanders of 228th and 229th squadron, Captains Enzo Stefani and Umberto Camera, and Second Lieutenant Cojana) were shot down by the Spitfires, while another three, seriously damaged, were forced to land on makeshift airfields.

Optimistically, the bomber gunners credited themselves with shooting down as many as six enemy fighters, including British Spitfires and American P.40s, while according to today's records, the attack on the 32nd Wing's S. 84 was carried out, without losses, by the Spitfire Vs of the 81st and 242nd Squadrons. The interception, which was largely credited to pilots of the 242nd Squadron, in particular Staff Sergeant G.A. Couttes and J.R. Sergeant Mallison, ten American Spitfires of 52nd Squadron also took part, although they were less effective than the British, since only their commander, Lieutenant Colonel Graham W. West, reported damaging one of the Italian bombers.

On the afternoon of 1 December, at 4:30 p.m., Supermarina requested Superaereo to ask the II Fliegerkorps Command to bomb the airfields in the area between Bona and Bougie during the night, in order to prevent enemy planes from taking off to attack the convoys. The II Fliegerkorps replied that 18 bombers (six Ju. 88s, two Do. 217s and ten He. 111s) were allocated for night operations against the airfields.

▲ The cruiser *Aurora*, flagship of the Q Force, taken in December 1942.

▲ The British destroyer *Ithuriel*, of Force Q, which was hit by a bomb at Bona on 1 December 1940 and was stranded there.

▼ In the centre Rear Admiral Edward Venables-Vernon-Harcourt, commander of the 12th Division and Force Q, with two captains of the cruisers under him. At right William Gladstone Agnew, co-commander of the Aurora, Harcourt's command ship.

THE DEPARTURE FROM BONA OF FORCE Q AND THE APPROACH TO CONVOY H (AVENTINO)

The port of Bona, with its excellent docks and unloading facilities, had become in the second half of November 1942 the forward base for supplies of General Kenneth Arthur Noel Anderson's 1st British Army, which operated on the border with Tunisia, occupied by Axis forces. The northern front line was then in the Tabarca area. Bona, on the border between Tunisia and Algeria, was also equipped with a good airfield and being within range of the enemy routes from Italy to Tunis and Bizerte, it was well placed to attack the enemy's supplies, with night raids by cruisers and destroyers.

Thanks to Ultra's decryptions at Bletchley Park (Government Code and Cypher School) on 22 November, the British realised that some Italian convoys were on the move for Tunis, Bizerte and Tripoli and, in order to intercept them, they transferred Rear Admiral Edward Venables-Vernon-Harcourt's Force Q, commander of the 12th Division on the cruiser *Aurora,* from Algiers to Bona. In addition to the *Aurora,* armed with six 152 mm guns, the Q Force included two other light cruisers of the 'Dido' class, the *Sirius* and *Argonaut,* both with ten 133 mm rapid-fire guns, and two modern destroyers, the British *Quentin* and the Australian *Quiberon,* each with four 120 mm guns.

In November-December 1941, the *Aurora's* commander, Captain William Gladstone Agnew, had led as commodore the famous Malta K Force, consisting of the cruisers *Aurora* and *Penelope* and the destroyers *Lance* and *Lively.* In November 1941, it had sunk thirteen merchant ships of the convoys 'Duisburg', 'Maritza', 'Aventino' and 'Montanari' destined to supply Libya, and two escort units, the destroyers *Libeccio* and *Da Mosto,* leading to a crisis in the Regia Marina that was only overcome by the arrival in Sicily of Field Marshal Albert Kesselring, Hitler's top aviation commander, who also appointed him as Oberbefehlshaber Süd (Oberbefehlshaber Süd - OBS). Dependent on the 2nd Air Fleet (2nd Luftflotte) were the 2nd and 10th Air Corps (II and X Fliegerkorps), respectively stationed in Italy and Greece, the Kriegsmarine Command in Italy and also the Afrika Korps of General, later Field Marshal, Erwin Rommel. Reporting to Romme4l, for support of land operations in Libya and Tunisia, were the air units of the Air Command Africa (Fliegerführer Afrika) and the Air Command Tunis (Fliegerkorps Tunis), which still depended on the OBS.

Naturally the Italians and Germans were aware of Bona's value, both as an arrival point for supplies for the Army in Tunisia and as a base for the Royal Navy's light units, cruisers and destroyers. And therefore the Axis air forces, starting with bombers from the airfields and airfields from Sicily and Sardinia and with dive-bombers also from Tunisia, carried out violent and daily day and night attacks throughout November 1942. Particularly violent were the raids on the night of 27/28, which lasted for five and a half hours, causing, among other things, severe damage to the destroyer *Ithuriel* (Lieutenant Commander David Hugh Maitland-Makgill-Crichton) which, attacked while preparing to go out to sea with the other units of Force Q, was hit in the middle by a bomb and run aground, was con-

▲ Rear Admiral Cecil H.J. Harcour, commander of the 12ᵗʰ Division inspects a representative of the cruiser *Argonaut* in Algiers, accompanied by the commander, Captain Eric William Longley Cooky, who is following him.

▼ The cruiser *Aurora*, flagship of the Q Force, filmed at Bona in December 1942.

sidered a 'total loss' and therefore not repairable. She was decommissioned in November 1945.

It should also be mentioned that British submarines, from the 8th Gibraltar Squadron and the 10th Malta Squadron, were continuously patrolling along the routes of Axis convoys, and in particular were stationed in ambush near the ports of Tunis and Bizerte; which forced the Supreme Command of the Italian Armed Forces, under the command of Chief of Staff General Marshal Ugo Cavallero, to organise, with the help of the OBS, a continuous anti-submarine patrol in the area between western Sicily and Tunisia, with the use of light naval units and aircraft.

The O.I.C./M.C.183 dispatch of 29 November to the Q Force reported:

"Steamers PUCCINI, AVENTINO, GUALDI, tanker GIORGIO and K.T.1 will set sail from Palermo at 06.30 a.m. on the 1st, their departure having been delayed by 24 hours, joining up with the ASPROMONTE off Trapani and then heading for Tunisian ports at a speed of 9 knots. The GUALDI and GIORGIO for Tunis and the others for Bizerte. Both convoys are likely to arrive at 06.00 hrs on day 2. (Q Force)'.

The arrival in Bizerte of the steamers *Arlesiana, Achille Lauro, Campania* and *Menes,* travelling at 7 knots, was scheduled at 11.00 am on 2 December; the one bound for Tripoli, Convoy C, with the steamers *Chisone* and *Veloce,* and a speed of 9 knots, would set sail at 8.30 pm on 3 December. [6]

The three convoys were sighted by RAF scouts on the afternoon of 1 December, and at 17.30 Force Q sailed from Bona to surprise them west of the Sicilian Channel. Harcourt's instructions to the five commanders were as follows:[7]

"(a) Keep in line so that any ship outside the line [can be] *clearly* [identified as] *enemy.*

b) Bring the action to a head, attack the escort first and then the convoy, the flagship will signal the escort unit to attack by pointing its bow in its direction.

c) Only use illuminants if visibility does not allow you to see the drop points.

d)In the event of strong separation from the line, signal your position with the scrum lights.

e) Up to the start of the action, signal only with the light dimmed in line with method F.

f) Maintain absolute radio silence during the approach.

(g) In cases of absolute necessity, only radio signals limited to the horizon are permitted, so as not to allow radio interception by the enemy.' [8]

The five Q Force units complied with these navigation and attack regulations, with one exception, as we shall see, for a short time during the mission.

---

6 *Ibid*, Appendix VI, p. 329.
7 AUSMM, *Exchange of news with British Admiralty*, Enclosure I to HSL 99/57.
8 The note stated: 'It was *later found that R/F messages on V.H.F. could be detected on the radiogoniometer*'.

▲ The British cruiser *Argonaut*, one of Force Q's units, at Bona in December 1942. Note the work in progress to repair the damage caused to the harbour docks by Axis aircraft attacks. Below: profile of a 'Dido' class cruiser. Force Q had two of them, Sirius and *Argonaut*.

▼ The torpedo boat *Partenope*, which together with its twin *Perseo* preceded the convoy route to Tunis and Bizerte for anti-ship, anti-submarine and dredging surveillance.

To ward off possible enemy sightings, until sunset Force Q headed west, and at 18.00 she reversed course to 052°, proceeding in the darkness at the remarkable speed of 27 knots, with the units in line, in order *Aurora* (Lieutenant-Captain William Gladstone Agnew), *Sirius* (Lieutenant-Captain Patrick William Beresford Brooking), *Argonaut* (Lieutenant-Captain Eric William Longley-Cook), *Quiberon* (Lieutenant-Captain Hugh Waters Ahelley Browning), *Quentin* (Lieutenant-Captain Allan Herbert Percy Noble). While underway, at 20.45 and 22.10, the *Aurora* received a report from a night reconnaissance aircraft of the presence of convoy H, also known as convoy 'Aventino' after the command ship's name. On the basis of the first report of convoy H at 21.00, with Force Q standing at lat. 37°50'N, long. 09°00'E corresponding to 22 miles by 360° from La Galite Island, the formation's course was changed for 104°, speed 27 knots. This followed an assessment made on the *Aurora,* in which it was assumed that an enemy convoy, perhaps two, would reach a point at midnight 2 miles by 053° from the position where the cruiser would be.

At 23.03 the Bengali aircraft, which until then had been intermittently illuminating the convoy, received the order, intercepted by the Italian listening stations, '*do not illuminate the enemy*'. *It* was believed that the signal was made by the British '*evidently in order to avoid as much as possible the sighting of their own ships by the convoy*'.[9]

At 11.30 p.m., two objects appeared on the *Aurora*'s Type 271 radar screen about 4 miles to the south, and it was thought that they might be two enemy Mas (in English MTBs), while in reality they might also be the two Italian torpedo boats *Partenope* and *Perseo* proceeding the course of the Italian convoys H and B, dredging the route and keeping an anti-som sound on the echogoniometer.

The Q Force held its course for 104°, because it was not considered possible that under those conditions, the Mas could have successfully attacked the naval formation.

According to the torpedo boat *Partenope*'s report, after the glare of anti-aircraft and illuminating fire had been sighted from astern, at 11.35 p.m. an enemy aircraft was overflown, and at 11.48 p.m. a black silhouette was sighted '*for 45° to starboard of the bow*'. The *Partenope*'s commander, Lieutenant Commander Gustavo Lovatelli, after making the prescribed recognition signal to which the torpedo bomber did not respond, took no initiative to signal this presence to the air, probably because he knew that the position of the torpedo motorboats at sea was known. [10]

Meanwhile, at 23.37 hrs, flashes were seen from aboard the Q Force ships for 078°, at a distance of about 20 miles. At the same time the sky began to cloud over and heavy downpours followed at intervals.

---

9 AUSMM, Supermarina, *Naval clash on the night of 2 December.*

10 From Supermarina's Diary, we know that during the night of 2 December, three Italian motor torpedo boats, which left from Bizerte, participated in the landing of 150 men of the San Marco Regiment on the Galite islands, which was occupied without resistance. It then appears that German motor torpedo boats of the 3rd Flotilla, which set sail from Bizerte at 00.01 a.m. on 2 December, spent the night 'in the area of *Cape Coram for an anti-landing ambush*' in the area of Tabarca, where land fighting was taking place between German and British forces on the border of Tunisia with Algeria.

At 00.01 a.m. on 2 December 1942, being in lat. 37°32'N, long. 10°35'E, the Q Force set course 050°, and speed was reduced to 25 knots. One minute later seven flashes were sighted on bearing 050°, at a distance of 15 miles. Heading towards the point where the British Air-to-Surface Vessel (ASV) radar reconnaissance aircraft were illuminating the target with flares, at 00.21 hrs echoes between 040° and 080° appeared on the radar screens, at distances of 3 to 6 miles, and as it was evident that a convoy would soon be encountered, the *Aurora*, changed course for 040° and reduced speed further to 20 knots.

At 00.36 the *Aurora*, lying lat. 37°39° N, long. 10°50'E, corresponding to 60 miles north of Bizerte, sighted two ships and manoeuvred to attack them.[11] As we shall see later in detail, in a firing action that lasted for an hour until 01.35, convoy H was completely destroyed.

In fact the movement of the British ships towards the Sicilian Channel had not gone unnoticed. Force Q had been sighted at 22.40 on 1 December at 60 miles by 290° from Cape Bon by a German Ju. 88 reconnaissance plane of Squadron 2.(F)/122, which reported: *"2240 - 5 unspecified warships of medium tonnage - High speed - course 90 in 37°42' - 09°45'"*.[12] The sighting point of the enemy formation proceeding on a Levant course corresponded to 20 miles north of Bizerte.

Recorded at 10.40 p.m., the news of the sighting was, however, not transmitted by Supermarina to the OBS until an hour later (11.44 p.m.), a circumstance underlined by the subsequent Report on the annihilation of the '*Aventino*' convoy written by Admiral Angelo Parona, commander of the 3rd Naval Division in Messina[13] . Parona wrote that the reasons for the delay were ignored, angering the Chief of Staff of the Regia Marina, Admiral Arturo Riccardi, who ordered him to '*eliminate those considerations that were outside the limits of the task*' he had received. According to Riccardi, the delay was not Supermarina's fault, but Superaereo's, because '*the sighting aircraft, having a malfunctioning radio,* [had] communicated *the discovery only on its return and this* [had] reached *Supermarina by telephone only at 2330*'. In fact, examination of the German documents did not confirm the alleged failure of the aircraft's radio.

As stated in a memorandum from Supermarina, compiled by Captain Lorenzo Gasparri, Commander of the Destroyer Group of the Naval Squadron, which confirmed at 23.30 the arrival time of the discovery signal transmitted by the OBS, the operational body of the Naval High Command made the following assessment of the situation: [14]

---

11 Ibid. Supermarina radio stations intercepted the sighting report at 00.33 that convoy H was *"3 miles by 70°"* from the unit that had sighted it. It must also be said that Force Q's course was 104° and not 90° as reported by the German aircraft. The attack, according to Italian reports, took place at lat. 37°40'N, long. 10°58'E.

12 In an OBS memo, sent on 2 December 1942 to Supermarina and with the subject *"Orientation on the situation at sea"*, it is reported: *"2240 - 5 supposed medium-ton warships (later reported as 1 Incr. and 5 CC.TT), sighted by one of our aircraft in 9843/03 East, course East, high speed"*. The report of the presence of a cruiser and five destroyers came when the naval combat had been over for several hours. This news, brought to Supermarina's attention by the German Navy Command in Italy, which resided in premises adjacent to those of the Regia Marina High Command's operational organ, and which had been relayed by the German Navy Command in Tunisia, read: '*Airplane report: Enemy formation would be composed, at 01.40 hours, at 37°37'N, 11°15'E, of one cruiser and five destroyers*'. See, Hand Message No. 256 of 2 December 1942.

13 AUSMM, *Clash on the night of 2 December 1942 south of the Skerki Bank between enemy naval forces and convoy 'Da Recco'*, Annex to sheet no. 449/SRP of 12 December 1942-XXI.

14 AUSMM, '*Report of the events relating to the action that took place on the night of 1 to 2 December 1942 about 38 miles

'The discovery signal was immediately launched and transmitted by the r.t. station at 23.40'.

Examination of the situation revealed the following:

- Convoy C was considerably isolated from the range of the sighted forces.

- convoy G had already been attacked by aircraft and the tanker GIORGIO, which had been hit, was on fire from 225001.

- Convoys H and B were those most directly threatened and in particular H which was not only more advanced than the other, but also followed a route of most likely encounter with enemy units. Attributing to the latter a speed of 30 knots (which later turned out to be the actual speed) it appeared very likely that the convoy would be sighted between 001002 and 003002.

In the meantime, the O.B.S. had asked if it was to be supposed that the forces sighted at 224001 were national; Supermarina replied that this seemed to be ruled out because only three M.S. were sailing that night between Bizerte and La Galite. However, the O.B.S. was asked to give some less uncertain information as to the type of ships sighted and whether the sighting could be referred to M.S..

The O.B.S. replied that given the time at which the sighting took place, it was not possible to provide more precise information, but that it could not be ruled out that the units sighted were M.S. either.

However, given the position and course of the sighted force, Supermarina judged that they must be adversary units; therefore, having asked the O.B.S. to attack them, Supermarina gave her consent after accurately reporting the position and course of convoys B and H and drawing the O.B.S.'s attention to the need to avoid misunderstandings.

Immediately after the transmission of the discovery message, it was examined whether it was expedient to order the reversal of convoys B and H.

Bearing in mind that diversion orders given to convoys are generally not executed until 30 or even 45 minutes after the order has been given, it was observed that if the enemy force had the speed of about 30 knots, it would have arrived in the area of convoy H while the reversal manoeuvre was in progress; in any case, tactical contact between the adversary forces and convoy H would have been delayed by very little, given the relative positions that both groups must have had.

It therefore still appeared preferable that convoy H and its escort units should be in an orderly formation when the sighting was imminent. Therefore the order to turn or change course to convoy H was not given'.

Finally, it should be mentioned that at 11.40 p.m. on 1 December, i.e. exactly one hour after the sighting of the Q Force heading east, another German reconnaissance plane reported, without specifying the time of sighting: "*6 light units Rv. 90° 20 mgl. north of Bizerte.* This was the same British naval formation, which was heading on convoy H.

---

for 350° from Cape Bon'.

▲ The torpedo boat *Perseo* in 1942.

The same behaviour was held in Rome with regard to convoy B, which at 01.00 was about 60 miles behind convoy H, as it was considered that the escort commander, Captain Aldo Cocchia, *"having received the discovery message transmitted by Supermarina at 234001 and the subsequent one from DA RECCO"*, which at 0030 had transmitted a signal requesting orders regarding the sighting of the German aircraft at 22.40, *"could have adjusted in the most opportune way in relation to his position with respect to that of convoy H"*. And in fact at midnight, convoy B, on the initiative of its commander, turned left on course 80° heading for Palermo.

As can clearly be seen, these were the real reasons why the turnaround of convoy H and B was not ordered after the German air sighting. And with this memo, Supermarina took full responsibility, bringing to light operational shortcomings that were unfortunately forgotten in the post-war period by dealing with the subject in the Official History, ambiguously reporting only what did not appear compromising for the prestige of the Navy.

Since Force Q's attack, according to Italian reports in agreement with British ones, began at 00.36, Supermarina had at least an hour to order if not the hijacking then at least the splitting up of the convoy. Evidently, as stated in the Memorandum, Supermarina had underestimated what the actual threat was and, believing that only destroyers, and therefore relatively less dangerous ships than cruisers, might attack, it did not take the necessary more rational measures.

I would point out that, due to the urgency of dealing with the enemy threat, the order to divert the convoy H's change of course or dispersal could have been transmitted to the destroyer *Da Recco* promptly in clear and conventional language, and also by radio, which would have saved a great deal of time. It is not certain that the merchant ships in the convoy, due to their low speed of 10 knots, could evade pursuit by the enemy ships, but at least it could be attempted, and had they split up in the darkness some of them would have passed or turned back.

In fact, as appears from Memo No. 125 of 3 December 1942, sent to the Supreme Command and consequently to the attention of the Head of the Government, Benito Mussolini, Supermarina, confirming his doubts about that sighting of the German aircraft, and perhaps not knowing how to justify his irrational decision, wrote: [15]

'The AVENTINO convoy was part of a split system of four convoys, all moving at the same time in the night on the 2nd. The mere news of the Bona presence of war units could not have been enough to make the already very advanced operation stop, given the extreme urgency of it.

If you had to counter-send transport operations and reroute convoys every time you receive the first news of a sighting, which is often unconfirmed, or when the presumed presence of the enemy in an area makes it possible for them to intervene, the traffic would certainly be safer, but far less intense. And fuel consumption would become prohibitive.' [16]

As we have seen, in Supermarina's assessment, 'convoy G (Palermo - Tunis), reported by British scouts, had been attacked south of Marettimo at 9.15 pm. The torpedo hit tanker *Giorgio was on* fire and immobilized, having her two escort units, the destroyer *Lampo* and the torpedo boat *Climene*, close by.

Convoys H and B were the ones that appeared to be most directly threatened, and of these, convoy H in particular, because apart from being in the most advanced position, it was also the one that was most likely to encounter enemy units, which it could have sighted between 00.10 and 00.30 on 2 December.

Also at 00.30, the destroyer *Da Recco*, the lead escort unit of convoy H, transmitted a signal requesting orders in connection with the 10.40 p.m. aerial sighting, about which there was evidently concern. But before a reply could be received, at 00.40 the *Da Recco* transmitted a signal to discover enemy units.

Meanwhile, while Supermarina was deciding what to do, at 00.25 on 2 December, the OBS had informed Superaereo: *'The Germans will attack the five units sighted north of Bizerte with bombers during the night and with torpedo bombers at dawn.*

But let us see how the attack by the British units and the destruction of the merchant ships of Convoy H came about.

---

15 AUSMM, *Consideration of the naval action on the night of 2 December 1942-XX.*

16 Regarding the necessity of escorting convoys with the main naval forces, which was then mainly the German charges, in Memo No. 125, Supermarina wrote: "*A Naval Division stationed in Cagliari would have made it possible not to prevent naval action, but to bind it with the possibility of a rendezvous at dawn.* And this was due to the need to prevent a night encounter in which the Italian Navy was not sufficiently trained, and at the same time lacked equipment suitable for that type of combat, such as radar and optical sighting apparatus with a large night light.

▲ Visit to the cruiser *Trieste* in Messina by General Bruno Loerzer, Commander of the 2nd Fliegerkorps in Sicily. From left, Vice Admiral Angelo Parona, Commander of the 3rd Cruiser Division, Loerzer, Captain Renato Salvatori, Commander of the *Trieste*, and two other officers.

▼ The cruiser *Sirius*. Like the *Dido* and *Argonaut* it belonged to the 'Dido' class, and had a formidable naval and anti-aircraft armament with 10 high-elevation, high-cadence 133 mm naval and anti-aircraft guns.

▲ The 'Navigatori' class destroyer *Nicoloso Da Recco*, command ship of convoy H ('*Aventino*').

▼ Wartime navigation of an Italian torpedo boat. The two forward 100 m/m cannons are held ready to fire at the maximum elevation of 45°.

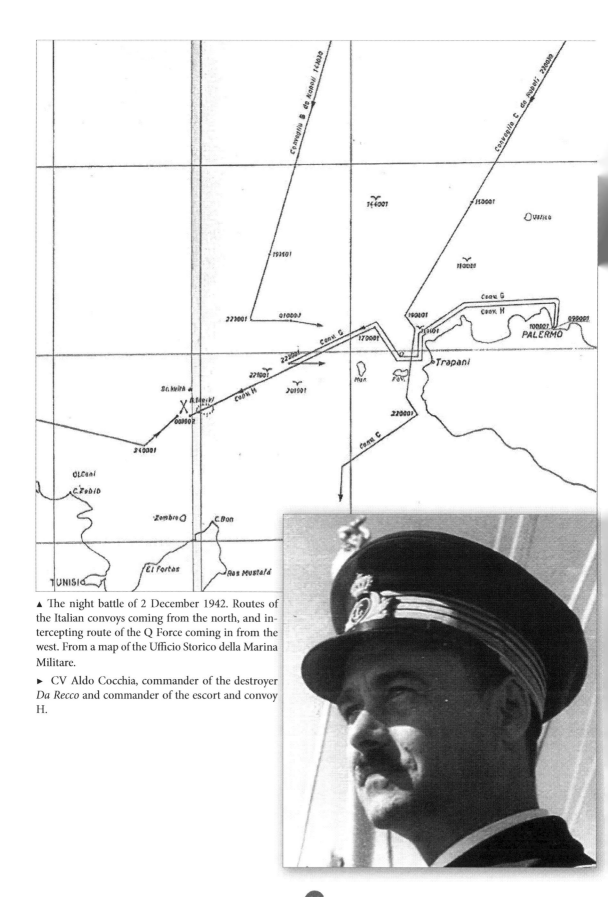

▲ The night battle of 2 December 1942. Routes of the Italian convoys coming from the north, and intercepting route of the Q Force coming in from the west. From a map of the Ufficio Storico della Marina Militare.

► CV Aldo Cocchia, commander of the destroyer *Da Recco* and commander of the escort and convoy H.

THE NAVIGATION OF CONVOY H UNTIL THE ENCOUNTER WITH FORCE Q

After leaving Palermo at 10.15 a.m. on 30 December, Convoy H, marching at a speed of 10 knots, had assumed a sailing formation with the merchant ships in two columns, protected by escort units (see map below).

The steamers *Aventino* and *Aspromonte,* spaced 800 metres apart, were, in relation to the direction of course, on the left column, the *Puccini* and *K.T. 1,* equally spaced apart, on the right column. The distance between the two columns was also 800 metres. Two escort units, the destroyer escort ship *Da Recco* (sea captain Aldo Cocchia) was 1,700 metres to the left of the *Aventino,* but about 800 metres ahead, and was followed, at a distance of 1,600 metres, by the torpedo boat *Clio,* which was 1,500 metres away parallel to the last ship in the convoy column, the *Aspromonte.* Arranged equally were, on the right flank of the steamer *Puccini* and K.T.1, the *torpedo* boat *Procione* followed by the destroyer *Camicia Nera.* In a position 1,000 metres behind the centre of the convoy columns was the destroyer *Folgore,* which, in the event of a turnaround, following a naval threat alarm, would be in a suitable position to conceal the steamers with fog curtains, and also be in a suitable position to counterattack.[17]

In the order of operation drawn up by Captain Cocchia and brought before departure from Palermo to the knowledge of the commanders of the ships of convoy H and the escort, it was stipulated that, in the event of an encounter with surface units:[18]

"The escort torpedo boats will attack the *enemy, engaging him thoroughly and covering the convoy with fog. Merchant units will take, even without orders, the fastest route away, trying to cover themselves with fog. FOLGORE and CLIO will stay with the convoy.*

These directives were discussed at the meeting with the commanders of all ships of convoy H, which took place on the escort destroyer *Da Recco,* and which Commander Aldo Cocchia described as follows in his autobiographical book[19]

"On 30 November, I summoned the commanders of the warships and merchant ships for the customary meeting held before each departure. The meeting was particularly large because I also invited the communications officers of the individual units to attend, to whom I wanted to give personal instructions, as I considered the service they would be reporting to be so essential. I gave the usual directives for encounters with enemy aircraft and submarines, prescribed the various formations to be used, the signals that would be exchanged, and specified that if enemy surface ships were sighted, DA RECCO, CAMICIA NERA and PROCIONE would go on the attack without waiting for orders or signals and would fight to the bitter end; *in such an eventuality the merchant ships would have taken, accompanied by FOLGORE and CLIO, the fastest route away, also without awaiting orders'.*

---

17 The running chart, both day and night of the convoy, was that provided for in articles 18 and 19 of the D.T.1S. edition of July 1942.
18 AUSMM, R. C.T. Da Recco, *Operation Order No. 17,* 30 November 1942.
19 Aldo Cocchia, *Convoys. Un marinaio in guerra 1940-1941*, Mursia, Milan, 2004, p. 299 ff.

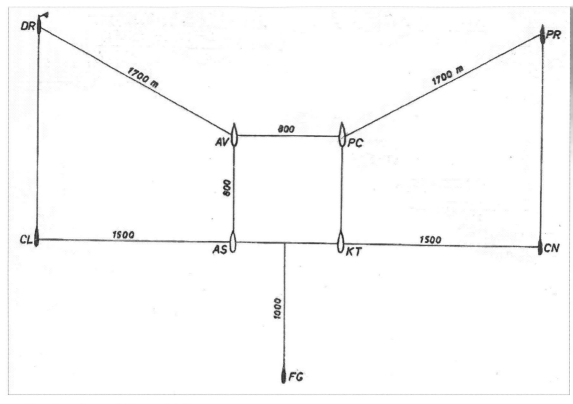

▲ Chart from the Naval Historical Office.

▼ The motor vessel *Puccini*, which collided with the *Aspromonte* and caused a dispersal of convoy H and escort ships shortly before the attack by Force Q began.

Convoy H's navigation during the night took place in calm seas, but also with very poor visibility, as the horizon was somewhat hazy and the moon was covered by thick cloud banks. There were no alarms until after 8 p.m. on 1 December, when until midnight, the convoy, which was proceeding on an east-southeast (245°) course, was continually over-flown, without attack, by aircraft that intermittently illuminated it with flares.[20] As a precaution, the merchant ships doubled the distance between the columns, while the escort units decreased it by moving closer to the side of the steamers in order to make masking with fog more effective, in case of attack.

Not so lucky was convoy G. After departing Palermo at 09.15 a.m. on 1 December, the tanker *Giorgio* (military commander Lieutenant Italo Cappa), escorted by the destroyer *Lampo* and the torpedo boat *Climene*, at 15.00 had turned course to await convoy H, which was to overtake her, and at 16.30, when this happened, as per the order of operations she followed the convoy itself, returning to her original course and keeping a few miles behind. At 6:33 p.m., having heard the sound of aircraft, measures were taken to deal with a possible attack. From 20:31 to 21:48 convoy G was continually overflown by planes, forcing the ships to frequent turns, making smoke and on occasion firing machine guns.

At 9.58 p.m., prepared by the firing of several flares on the port side, a number of planes were seen passing very close by and soon afterwards the *Giorgio* was hit by a torpedo on the bow, at tank No. 1, south of Marettimo Island and 44 miles by 268° from Trapani.

The aerial attack was carried out by three Albacore torpedo bombers of the 828th Squadron of the British Naval Aviation (Fleet Air Arms - FAA) which took off from the Maltese airport of Hal Far under the command of Lieutenant R.M. Maund and guided by another Albacore of the 821st Squadron by means of the ASV naval detection radar, which was also used as a bengalier aircraft. Lieutenant-Lieutenants Pratt and Kendrick, pilots of the Albacore, claimed that a torpedo had hit and set fire to a 6-7,000 tonne tanker, which was attacked at 22.55 hours 15 miles south of Marettimo.

Meanwhile, to attack the same convoy at 19.25, another formation of seven Albacore from the FAA's 221st Squadron, five torpedo bombers and two Benghaziers had taken off from Malta; but the crews failed to locate the enemy ships.

Following the torpedo explosion, a violent blaze broke out on the *Giorgio* tanker, which also hit the bridge, and a major fire broke out in the bow area of the ship, while the machinery broke down, resulting in orders to extinguish the boiler to prevent a possible further fire. While the wounded were being rescued, the tanker *Giorgio came to a* halt, lurching to starboard and somewhat dishevelled, and the two escort units, the destroyer *Lampo* and the torpedo boat *Climene,* came to her rescue.

---

20 At 19:56 on 30 November, the destroyer *Folgore*, the only ship in convoy H equipped with the radar wave detector 'Metox', reported to the command ship *Da Recco* '*We have been located by aircraft*'. When asked the distance to the enemy aircraft, the *Folgore* transmitted that the aircraft was approaching, but the distance was not known. From the destroyer *Da Recco,* the ships in the convoy were then ordered to '*Stand by for fog*'. In the following minutes, to the Squadron Leader's various requests to be informed about the "Metox" readings, the *Folgore* replied that the enemy plane "*was always overhead*".

▲ The Italian tanker *Giorgio*, which was hit and damaged by a torpedo dropped from a British Albacore aircraft of the 828th Squadron based in Malta, at Hal Far Naval Airfield.

Meanwhile, as the convoy 'Aventino' continued sailing, with the burning of the *Giorgio* tank clearly visible from astern, the destroyer escort *Da Recco* deciphered the signal for the discovery of force Q, transmitted by Supermarina at 23.40, which was followed by another signal at 23.30, ordering him to assign a torpedo boat to dredge the convoy's bow, which was approaching a heavily mined area, with barrages in an unfamiliar position.

Commander Cocchia assigned the *torpedo* boat *Procione to* this manoeuvre with the order to "*well ahead*", and at the same time, in order to guard against a possible enemy naval attack, he asked Supermarina to move the convoy about 3 miles to the south; a manoeuvre which Commander Cocchia ordered all ships to do at 00:05 on December 2nd, after they had sighted flares ahead to present the stern to the light curtain. This was followed by a 90° turn to port, and then resumed the normal course after another turn at 00.17 on the starboard side.

But this double manoeuvre completely disrupted the formation, as the motor vessel *Puccini*, not having received the signal for the second course deviation at 00.17, hit the steamer *Aspromonte*. The *Puccini* stayed behind, and the same happened to the *Aspromonte, which was* forced to stop for a few minutes.[21] On the other hand, the German steamer K.T. 1, manoeuvring in the wake of the *Puccini*, being the only ship without ultra-short-wave radio apparatus that allowed for speech, and also lacking a beacon despite being a very modern ship, instead of turning 150°, had probably continued on a 245° course, at the same time increasing its speed to 12 knots, the maximum it could develop. This hypothetical consideration stems from the fact that *K.T. 1*, following the Q Force attack, was never heard from again.

---

21 Without the Italian ships noticing anything, at 21.55 on 1 December Convoy H was sighted by the British submarine *Seraph*, which together with the *Sibyl* had been sent to the area where the Italian convoys bound for Tunisia were expected to pass. Having begun the surface pursuit, with the Italian ships being illuminated by flares fired by British aircraft, and having come to the surface at 00.01 a.m. on the 2nd, at 00.07 a.m. the *Seraph* attacked with two salvoes of three bow torpedoes a merchant ship of convoy H, believed to be 5,000 tons, and the commander, Lieutenant of the Navy, Norman Limbury Auchinleck Jewell, felt it had been hit with a torpedo, one minute and 35 seconds after the "*out*". The Italian ships heard two underwater explosions, believed to be caused by bombs, and a few minutes later the Aspromonte and the Puccini collided.

However it was, the double misfortunate course change manoeuvre decided by Captain Cocchia, put the ships of the convoy, and in particular the escort ships, in the most difficult position to face the impending attack of the British units, with the Italian ships being in the process of rearranging their formation. The destroyer *Folgore* approached the *Puccini* to show him the course, the torpedo boat *Clio* was sent to assist the *Aspromonte*, whose commander announced that he could continue sailing. It was estimated that *K.T 1 was at* a distance of three and a half miles to the northwest of the destroyer *Da Recco, which was being* followed by *the Aventino* and had, still astern, at a distance of about 6,000 metres, a group of ships that had formed with the *Puccini, Aspromonte, Clio* and *Folgore*. Finally, the destroyer *Camicia Nera (Camicia Nera) was to the* west of the *Aventino* and the *torpedo* boat *Procione*, which was about to put to sea the paramine (divergents) was to be 2-3,000 metres ahead of the *Da Recco*.

These, as Commander Cocchia wrote in his report, were to a good approximation the positions of the Italian ships when, at 00.37 on 2 December under the Skerki Bank, '*the first salvo from one of the British ships departed*' (see map below), which, let us remember, were in a line, with the cruiser *Aurora in the* lead, followed in order by the *Sirius, Argonaut* and the CT *Quentin* and *Quiberon*.

Shortly before the attack began, which was fought with a series of detached actions made it difficult to describe exactly what the reciprocal naval movements were, the radio station of the destroyer *Da Recco* intercepted and then deciphered a discovery message sent over the air by a British unit with time group 003202, and compiled as follows "*Convoy sighted 3 miles by 70° my position lat. 37°41'N, long. 10°51'*". Upon sighting the enemy, at 00.40, the *Da Recco* transmitted the discovery signal on ultra-short wave, and by main radio.

▲ The CT *Folgore*, the first unit of the H convoy escort to go on the attack immediately after the sighted Q Force ships had opened fire.

▼ Navy Historical Office map. From top right: CM *Camicia Nera*, PC *Puccini*, FG *Folgore*, AS *Aspromonte*, CL *Clio*, AV *Aventino*, DR *Da Recco*, PR *Procione* KT *K.T.1*.

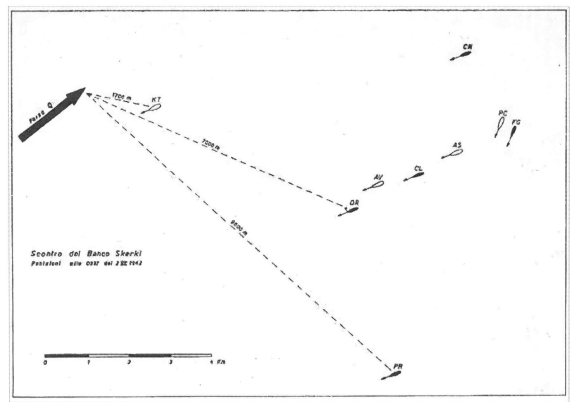

THE INITIAL PHASE OF THE ATTACK ON CONVOY H

As we have said, in explaining how Force Q's approach to Convoy H took place, the flagship cruiser *Aurora* under Captain Agnew, with Rear Admiral Harcourt on board, had sighted two ships at 00:36 on 2 December. First the silhouette of a small-ship appeared on the port bow, against which 152 mm guns were aimed, and then that of another small ship which was sighted a little further away. At 00.37 the course of the Q Force was altered to head against the second unit, and the cruisers *Aurora* and *Sirius, with their* guns aimed off the starboard bow, opened fire from a distance of 1,800 yards (1,700 m) against the 850 GRT steamer K.T. 1, which was hit by the first double broadside. At Rear Admiral Harcourt's request to the firing director, illuminating shells were fired to better illuminate the target. Also targeted, at 00.39, by a broadside from Captain Longley-Cook's cruiser *Argonaut*), which then fired a torpedo at *K.T. 1, it was* seen to swerve and sink within minutes, with the total loss of the men on board, along with four tanks, ten vehicles and 120 tons of various materials.

In the meantime, the *Argonaut* and the Australian destroyer *Quiberon* fired, on the starboard beam, at a light unit detected to the south-east, probably the *torpedo* boat *Procione* or the destroyer *Da Recco* since artillery salvos were seen falling very close from both units.

At 00.38 the *Aurora*, pulling slowly to starboard, began to lead the formation in search of convoy H, and between 00.39 and 01.00, as we shall see, all the Q Force ships engaged various targets.

Also at 00:39, Commander Cocchia, transmitting over ultra-short waves, ordered the *Camicia Nera* and the *Raccoon to 'go on the attack'*, a manoeuvre which Lieutenant Commander Ener Bettiga with the destroyer *Folgore* had already begun to carry out with commendable initiative and great aggressiveness. At the same time, the *Da Recco* transmitted to the merchant ships of convoy H to reverse course to the north, and at 00.40 he then proceeded, as was his duty, to report the enemy attack to Supermarina on both ultra-short wave and main radio. At the same time the *Da Recco* pulled in for Rv 290°, then north-west, towards the position where the *Camicia Nera was,* gradually increasing its speed, and two minutes later *'opened fire on the starboard side firing illuminants from complex No. 2 and pounding fire from the other* complexes'. [22]

Also at 00.40, the *Aurora* opened fire with its 152mm guns at a destroyer detected to the north-east at a distance of 4,000 metres. According to the Ufficio Storico della Marina Militare, there were no Italian ships on that side. It was therefore a blunder, unless the destroyer's position was different, as from Rear Adm. Harcout there was a merchant ship near the destroyer. [23] This could have been the torpedo boat *Clio* (Lieutenant Vito Asaro), which had the motor vessel *Puccini* nearby.

---

22 AUSMM, R.C.T. N. Da Recco, *Report on the fight on the night of 2 December 1942-XXI.*
23 HMS *Aurora*, Report, Protocol No. 241/E of 5 December 1942.

At the same time, Captain Longley-Cook's cruiser *Sirius* fired from the starboard bow at a steamer, which was the motor vessel *Puccini*, which the torpedo boat *Clio* was trying to conceal together with the steamer *Aventino* by laying curtains of fog, and then fired two shots with its 100 mm cannons at an enemy ship that had turned on a searchlight, which was then turned off.

In the meantime, at 00:39 and then at 00:43, the *Argonaut* opened fire on a destroyer, probably the *Camicia Nera*, which, having spotted the enemy units by the light of their artillery flashes, and believing them to be two destroyers heading for the convoy, was manoeuvring for the torpedo attack, and which, framed by several salvoes, was seen by the British to cover itself with fog as it moved away. At 00.42, the *Aurora*, shifting the fire of her 152 mm guns to the starboard side and firing at a range of 3,800 meters, also targeted the *Camicia Nera*, mistaking it, however, for a large merchant ship, which was seen hit and set on fire, and which was believed to have been the *Aspromonte*. At 00.43, the *Aurora*, from a distance of about 4,400 metres, *fired on the* port side with her 152s against the same *Camicia Nera, which was* covered with fog to disengage after making an initial launch of three torpedoes, and then shifted her fire to the starboard side against another unidentified unit, firing her secondary 102 mm pieces at a distance of about 5.500 metres. The Ufficio Storico della Marina Militare believed that the *Aurora*'s last target might actually have been the torpedo boat *Procione* or the destroyer *Da Recco*.[24]

▲ The German steamer *K.T. 16*. To the same type belonged the *K.T. 1* the first ship of the H convoy to be sunk by the fire of the three Q Force cruisers.

---

24 For the reconstruction of the combat, in addition to the report forwarded to the Naval Historical Office by the British Admiralty Historical Section, various British documents in the National Archives, at the ADM/199 fund, and the book by Admiral Giuseppe Fioravanzo, *The Defence of Traffic with North Africa. Dal 1o ottobre 1942 alla caduta della Tunisia*, USMM, Roma, 1964, p. 145-170.

▲ The British cruiser *Argonaut*, which together with the Aurora targeted the Italian destroyer-turned-torpedo boat *Camicia Nera* with its 133 mm guns.

▼ The torpedo boat *Procione* at anchor with its sister ship *Sirius* behind it.

▲ The *Camicia Nera* before camouflage. On 30 July 1943, with the fall of fascism, it was renamed *Artigliere*.

▼ CT *Folgore*'s attacking manoeuvre.

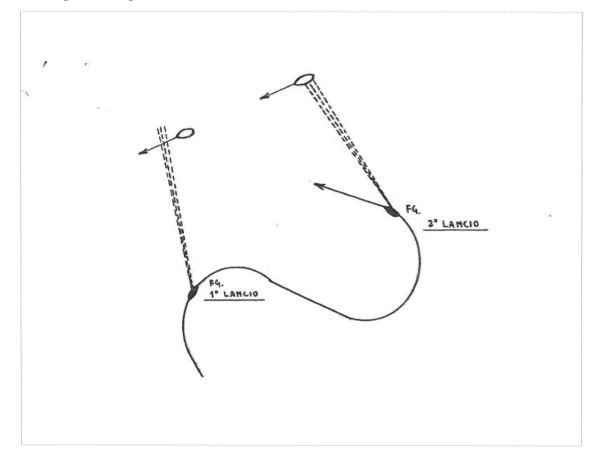

WHICH UNIT WAS ATTACKED BY THE DESTROYER CAMICIA NERA?

A careful reading of the reports on the battle finally makes it possible to clarify the embarrassing episode, hitherto passed over in silence, of which the *Camicia Nera* (frigate captain Adriano Foscari), the destroyer furthest to the north, was the protagonist. After immediately putting full speed to the torpedo attack to tighten the distance from the enemy destroyers, which were about 10° off port bow, making fog and slowing speed to 21 knots (so as not to be discovered with excessive bow wave and to better control the counter-boarding manoeuvre on the port side), at 00.43 the *Camicia Nera* fired a three torpedo salvo from about 2000 m on the units of the Forza Q which was making a slow turn to starboard. Some crew members thought that at least one torpedo had hit one of the enemy destroyers, but Commander Foscari realised that the salvo had missed.

The *Camicia Nera* was framed by several salvoes of 8 shots each [probably from one of the two "Dido" type cruisers, armed with ten 133 mm cannons, while the *Aurora* had six 152. mm cannons][25][2] but managed to evade enemy fire by pulling to starboard and moving away. As soon as he had finished the turn, Commander Foscari sighted a ship with two vertical funnels at about 800 m and, believing it to be a cruiser of the "Perth" type, he immediately directed for the attack, slipping alongside her from the stern at 34 knots and at 0034, he launched his three remaining torpedoes to starboard. As she turned away, the crew of the *Camicia Nera* saw two explosions on the enemy ship, a minor one in the stern and a major one in the middle, followed by a large fire and a huge burst, after which the ship seemed to disappear. The action of the *Camicia Nera*, still considered by historians and insiders to be of great fighting prowess, was at the time highly appreciated in military circles and exploited propagandistically by Benito Mussolini, who awarded frigate captain Adriano Foscari the Gold Medal for Military Valour, instead of the Silver Medal proposed by Supermarina.[26]

In reality, the Q Force suffered no losses or damage: the explosions and sinking of the 'enemy' unit were therefore merely a collective suggestion of the *Camicia Nera*'s crew and the second launch went as badly as the first. Besides, was the attacked unit really British? This one was isolated, whereas the British report shows that the Q Force had always remained in line. Isolated, on the other hand, was the Italian destroyer *Da Recco,* under the command of Captain Aldo Cocchia, which was heading eastward with the intention of outflanking the Q Force and attacking the trailing unit; and so the *Da Recco was to the* north of the enemy, which in turn was manoeuvring on a southerly course to the left of the '*Aventi-*

---

25 The final report of the *Camicia Nera*, was forwarded to Supermarina and other High Commands on 4 December 1942 with protocol no. 324/SRP, and with the subject "*Report on the action of 2 December 1942-XXI*. In it it is stated: "*At least two enemy units, valued for large CC.TT., can be glimpsed at about 10° to port bow, in line of detection with collusion course on the convoy. Manoeuvre to execute counter-board launch and at 0043 fire three torpedoes to port at an estimated range of 2000 m. (range 105°).*

26 The Commander of the Naval Squadron, Admiral Angelo Iachino, in a letter to Supermarina dated 24 December 1942, had proposed that Commander Foscari be awarded the Silver Medal for Military Valour along with promotion to Captain of the Navy for war merit.

no' convoy. The *Da Recco*'s commander had sighted an unknown destroyer off the bow and signalled to the torpedo tube operator to be "*careful*", but the torpedo launch had not been warned and therefore the destroyer did not carry out any evasive manoeuvre[27].

Despite the proposed decoration and advancement for frigate captain Foscari, in Rome they had immediately realised that the unit attacked by the *Camicia Nera* was the *Da Recco*: in fact, Supermarina put this in black and white in the Report on the *Clash during the night of 2 December 1942 south of the Skerki bank between enemy forces and the DA RECCO convoy*, sent on 29 December 1942, with protocol 35769. to Admiral Angelo Parona, in charge, as we have seen, of the investigation into the loss of convoy H:

"*The commanding officer sighted an enemy cruiser on the starboard side, which he appreciated was heading against the convoy. (This hypothesis must be discarded given the circumstances and the danger of a clash between the same enemy units that such a manoeuvre could have constituted. On the other hand, DA RECCO **shortly afterwards sees the enemy units in a single line of line and bearing)*". [boldface is by the author].

In the *Supplementary Report on the action of 2 December 1942-XXI*, forwarded, after a request for explanations, to Supermarina and the Maristat Training Office on 31 December 1942, Commander Foscari himself explained the reasons why he had ruled out the possibility that the unit attacked might have been the *Da Recco*:

"*At a certain moment (0055) the DA RECCO reported that he had "outflanked the enemy from the west and opened fire". This question of outflanking was not clear to me and, as I thought I had now passed beyond the enemy line of sight of the convoy, I had a kind of nightmare that I would find myself getting in the way of the DA RECCO, which I thought had also moved outwards. Shortly afterwards I saw an exchange of gunfire and I threw myself at full force to that side, without being able to understand who it was, all the more so because the one further to the west, which should have been, according to the above signal, the DA RECCO, was firing, it seemed to me, more heavily than one of our CTs could.*"[28]

Decisive to him, however, was the outline of the unit, which in the dark looked more imposing than that of a fighter. As a further puzzling clue, Commander Foscari added that some sailors had even spotted a third funnel, characteristic of the 'Emeralds':

"*The outline of the cruiser, for a distinctive sense of comparison with the CAMICIA NERA, appeared imposing: very long hull, high sides. Particularly striking to most observers, going from stern to bow, were two towers, an upright funnel with mast ahead, then a long, seemingly clear section, another funnel of more conspicuous size, and finally the not excessively*

---

27 AUSMM, Squadron CC.TT. Group Command, *Naval action of 2 December 1942*, prot. No. 04261 of 2 March 1943, addressed to Supermarina and for information to the Naval Squadron Command and Marina Messina. Also in Supermarina's report, *Scontro navale della notte del 2 dicembre*' (Naval *clash of the night of 2 December*), it is stated that the first attack of the *CAMICIA NERA* was against two destroyers and the second against a cruiser type 'Emerald', specifying that '*the enemy had to mistake the CAMICIA NERA for one of their own CC.TT. as they did not open fire against it*'.

28 In *Da Recco*'s report about the presence of the *CAMICIA NERA* in the vicinity, it is reported: "*0054 - The CAMICIA NERA reports having hit an enemy cruiser with a torpedo* [first attack]. *0100 - A C.T. is seen ahead. At the launch tubes attention. 0102 - BLACK CAMICIA is asked where the enemy is. The BLACK CHAMBER replies that he is on his starboard side. 0106 - the BLACK CHAMBER informs that the enemy is to the south of him and shortly afterwards informs that he has lost contact.*".

large command bridge. Some observers who could see the unit in a relatively different position would have seen a third funnel leaning against the bridge deck'.

Commander Foscari's report informs us that, having run out of torpedoes, the *Camicia Nera* sighted two other naval units on her bow; to disengage, she maneuvered north and then along various routes without encountering the enemy again. Taking course 50° at 01.14, it left the combat area, re-entering at 03.13 to give aid to the ships of the burning convoy. At 03.45 Foscari sighted and followed for some time a naval group which he believed to be composed of four units, one larger and three smaller ones, heading west.[29]³ These were certainly Italian ships, because the Forza Q, returning to Bona, was now far away and - as Supermarina noted - to be there at that time *"would have had to be sailing at 50 knots"*.[30]

Supermarina in fact gave no credence to the alleged successes of the *Camicia Nera*: the 9 June 1943 report on *Damage Inflicted on the Enemy*[31] also excludes the partial success of the first launch claimed by some sailors:

"The explosion of a torpedo on the enemy CT targeted by the first attack was not noticed by any officer, so the sighting by some sailors cannot be taken as the basis of an assessment, due to the ease with which in such circumstances a cannon salvo and torpedo flash can be mistaken for an explosion on board the enemy ship. ... There is a lack of any objective corroborating element'.

Certainly, after the war, they avoided raging over a mistake that had fortunately not had tragic consequences, so much so that the official history, written by Admiral Fioravanzo, dismisses the episode in only 11 lines without indicating what the targets of the attack were or making any comments:[32]

"The CAMICIA NERA (Capt. Adriano Foscari), which was the most northerly displaced CT... It immediately headed northwest, until at 0043 it launched three of its six torpedoes on the port side at an estimated distance of 2000 m (very close to the actual distance), which did not hit the Q Force which was making the slow turn to starboard. Immediately on the turning away course, she was framed by several salvoes of eight rounds each. As soon as he finished the turn, he fired the other three torpedoes to starboard at 00.45, which probably did not reach the target already moving away from the position occupied at that instant by the BLACK CAMICIA.

From the diagram of the *Camicia Nera*, attached to Commander Foscari's report, it is clear that at 00:45 on 2 December, the destroyer attacked with torpedoes a presumed cruiser, which was on her right with a northerly course, while the British units of the Q Force, against which she had made the first attack, were all in line on the left with a southerly course. Our reconstruction shows that the ship attacked was the *Da Recco*.

29 AUSMM, Supermarina, *Damage inflicted on the enemy*, Prot. No. 17480 of 9 June 1943.

30 AUSMM, *Clash on the night of 2 December 1942 south of the Skerki Bank between enemy naval forces and convoy 'Da Recco'*, Annex to sheet no. 35769 of 29 December 1942-XXI.

31 AUSMM, Supermarina, *Damage inflicted on the enemy*, Prot. No. 17480 of 9 June 1943.

32 Giuseppe Fioravanzo, *La difesa del traffico con l'Africa Settentrionale,* cit., p. 158 ff. Knowing Admiral Fioravanzo from the 1960s, and his volcanic character, I can imagine his disappointment at having to deal with a subject that was anything but an episode of great military value, to be proud of.

▲ The commando bridge and the single funnel of the *Folgore* destroyer.

▶ The British cruiser *Argonaut*, which sank the Italian destroyer *Folgore*.

▼ The forward part, from the bow to the funnel, of the *Folgore* destroyer.

THE ANNIHILATION OF THE AVENTINO CONVOY

Returning to Force Q's attack on convoy H, at 00.47 the cruiser *Sirius*, from a distance of 2 miles, fired from the port bow at two thin units, probably the destroyer *Folgore* and the torpedo boat *Clio* (which had seen the *Aspromonte* hit by enemy fire), and then at 00.53 carried out a brief firing action from the starboard bow against a small unit, which was probably the torpedo boat *Procione*.

The torpedo boat, which at the time the attack began had just completed the launching of the trailing cables (paramine), as it increased its speed towards the enemy, at 00:53 was immediately framed by artillery shells falling from the starboard bow, which the commander of the *Procione*, Lieutenant Commander Renato Torchiana, initially mistook for aeroplane bombs. Meanwhile, the trailing cables had to be cut, an operation that went on for a good twenty minutes, during which time the torpedo boat, still manoeuvring at high speed, remained under attack. Hit by pounding fire while deflecting on a northeast course along the enemy ships, the *Procione* was hit by two shells that caused heavy damage, and as the torpedo boat went to attack on the starboard side to launch torpedoes, she was hit again by three more shells and by numerous shrapnel shells that exploded near the hull.

Although the torpedo boat was full of dead and wounded, and from the leaks water entered the hull copiously, Commander Torchiana continued his attempt to launch the torpedoes. But this initiative was prevented by a rudder failure, caused by damage to his torpedo boat, which forced him, manoeuvring with the engines, to pull to the southwest, losing contact. The *Raccoon* finally continued sailing towards Tunis, no longer able to carry out any offensive action due to the impairment in her efficiency.

Aft on the left of the convoy, Lieutenant Commander Ener Bettiga's destroyer *Folgore* had meanwhile headed towards the flashes of gunfire and, after having deflected against the Q Force, at 00:44 came within 1,000/1,500 m of the *Aurora*, at the head of the enemy formation, launching, from the port side, an initial salvo of three torpedoes, and then pulling over to disengage. However, having sighted the cruiser *Sirius, which was* following the cruiser

Aurora and was illuminating a steamer with a searchlight, at 05.50 the *Thunderbolt*, after two approaches, to starboard and then to port, fired another salvo of three torpedoes at the *Sirius*, again from the port side, but once again without success, although the crew had the impression that they had hit two targets.

At 00.48 the *Argonaut* cruiser, the third unit in the British line, fired at an unidentified target 5,500 yards away, and four minutes later began firing eleven salvoes at the destroyer *Folgore*, which after the second torpedo run had taken a course to the east-south-east, continuing to pull to the left and open fire on enemy ships[33.] Nine shells hit the destroyer, causing fire and damage to vital parts.[34]

Struck by other shots, the *Folgore* continued to fire until it ran out of ammunition in its piece reserve, as it could not draw from the reserves due to the failures. In flames, the destroyer maneuvered for another 20 minutes to move away, with the intention of reaching Cagliari, the nearest national port; but despite moving with its engines at a certain speed, at 01:15, due to a heel that had reached 20 degrees due to water infiltration inside the hull, Commander Bettica, after hearing the opinion of Chief Engineer Mario Valvason, ordered the engines to stop. He then called the people on deck and ordered them to evacuate, while he remained on board. At 01.16 the destroyer *Folgore* sank with its heroic commander.

At 00.55 the *Aurora* cruiser signalled to the other Q Force units *"that its radar screen was clear to the south while there were still echoes to the north"*. So the cruiser *"pulled over to the left to locate them"*.

In the meantime, for two minutes, starting at 00.55, the destroyer *Quiberon*, briefly coming out of formation behind the *Argonaut*, fired from a distance of 4,600 metres at the torpedo boat *Clio*, sighted off the port beam, and recognised as a 'Sirius' type unit which, seen coming out of a smoke screen, was believed to be pulling in to fire torpedoes. It was believed that several shells had hit the target, while the water columns of some shells fired by the enemy unit were seen falling close astern and to the starboard of the *Quiberon*. In reality, the *Clio*, having sighted an enemy unit from astern at a distance of 4,500 metres, pulled to starboard and returned fire with her 100 mm cannons, managed to move away without being hit, developing a protective curtain of fog, thanks in part to the fact that the Australian unit, distracted by the false sighting of two non-existent Mas, at 01.01 she urgently pulled to starboard to avoid torpedoes, which the British report states were seen passing close to the Australian destroyer, on her port side.[35]

It is interesting what is reported in the Q Force Commander's report on the action of the destroyer *Quentin*, and its difficulties in firing while holding position and due to the lack of 120mm artillery shells without a flare.

---

33 At 00.48 hours, the torpedo boat *Clio, which was* keeping in sight of the steamers *Aventino* and *Puccini,* spotted a ship turning on a searchlight, which was turned off after a few seconds, and asked *Da Recco* if it was the enemy. The *Camicia Nera* replied in the affirmative. Then the *Clio* opened fire, firing two salvoes with the two forward guns from a distance of 4,500 metres. Shortly afterwards, he saw 'a *vessel proceeding south-east at very high speed with fire on board under the funnel'.* It was believed to be the *Thunderbolt,* which had not yet been hit.

34 In the Italian Report brought to the attention of the British Admiralty's Historical Section, it is reported that the *Folgore* was '*hit by enemy fire on both sides',* which gives the impression that, manoeuvring the ships of Force Q in a single line on the left, due to misrecognition of the target, Italian units which were on the right side of the enemy had also fired on the destroyer on the other side.

35 The *Quiberon* report contains the following annotation: '*Numerous targets were attacked during the action but, given the tail position of the formation, little remained to be done after the cruisers had passed'.*

▲ The Australian destroyer *Quiberon* engaged in combat with the torpedo boat *Clio*.

▼ The cruiser *Aurora* filmed from an aircraft while sailing in heavy seas.

"The QUENTIN, *after the QUIBERON left the formation, approached the stern of the Argonaut.*

It had difficulty keeping in contact because of the cordite smoke coming from the formation and the flashes from its forward guns. On numerous occasions, during course changes, the 'B' guns (just forward of the bridge) had to be ordered to cease fire. The report pointed out the urgent need for flameless ammunition. (It should be noted that ammunition for the 4.7 guns without muzzle flashes was being distributed but had not yet reached the QUENTIN)'.

Between 00.57 and 00.58, first the cruiser *Sirius* and then its twin *Argonaut* fired at the motor vessel *Puccini*, about 4,600 metres off the port bow. At 00.59 the same motor ship was illuminated by the cruiser *Aurora*, on the port bow. The target appeared in the light of the *Aurora*'s illuminating bullets as '*a lightly painted merchantman*', which was hit with nine 152 mm shells and set on fire. It must be said that, like the *Puccini*, the destroyer *Folgore*, on fire, also had the same light grey colour, and it is probable that it too may have been the target of the *Aurora* and the other two Force Q cruisers in the confused action, as the Ufficio Storico della Marina Militare was inclined to speculate.

At 01.00 hrs, the *Argonaut, which* had fired eight salvoes at the steamer *Puccini, fired* a torpedo at a burning ship and thought it had hit her on the port side. A minute later the *Sirius* also fired a torpedo at the same target, which was then seen to sink after two minutes. It was undoubtedly the steamer *Aventino* (Captain Giovanni Duili - military commander Lieutenant Commander Pietro Bechis), which had initially been illuminated by a searchlight and then, as mentioned, hit on the starboard side by violent and accurate fire from the *Argonaut.*

While reacting with her machine-guns, the *Aventino*, which at 3,794 gt was the largest ship in convoy H, had its command bridge, radio station, and rudder manoeuvring gear hit. In addition, the explosions from the bullets wreaked havoc among the men on board. The steamer, which was carrying 956 men of the Superga Infantry Division, 15 vehicles and 395 tons of various materials, immediately began to lurch to the left and to run aground. At 00.50 there was a violent explosion, which was rightly believed by Commander Bechis to be caused by a torpedo, we do not know whether launched from the *Argonaut* or the *Sirius; and* this led to an even more rapid sinking, which occurred at 00.50, causing the loss of many soldiers stowed in the lower rooms of the *Aventino*, and also the death of Commander Duili.

At 01.06, the *Quiberon* fired for four minutes on the *Puccini*, and this occurred while the Australian destroyer was passing through an area of shipwrecks in the water, those of the steamer *Aspromonte* which was in an imminent sinking condition. Nevertheless, the *Quiberon,* which had returned to formation at 01.10, manoeuvring together with the *Quentin*, resumed firing at 01.12 on the stationary and burning *Puccini*, stopping firing only after three minutes.

The motor ship *Puccini* (Captain Marcello Bulli - military commander Lieutenant Mario Vinelli), of 2,422 gt, carrying 810 men and 134 tonnes of various cargo, was hit by enemy fire on its starboard side and hit in the central area, where explosions and fires occurred, as it attempted to move away towards the east. The situation immediately appeared particularly critical, and the two commanders by mutual agreement ordered the thousand men on board to abandon ship. Many were already dead and many perished when, due to overloading, the lifeboats lowered into the sea capsized. Among those who perished were

▲ The steamer *Aventino*.

▼ Another pre-war image: the Ferrovie dello Stato ferry *Aspromonte* sailing in the Strait of Messina.

▲ The torpedo boat *Clio* in a pre-war image.

the two commanders of the *Puccini*, who, however, despite having the centre of the ship devastated and in flames, remained afloat until 3 p.m. on 2 December, when the destroyer *Camicia Nera*, having recovered thirty soldiers and an Army captain who had remained on board, gathered at the stern and, judging the motor vessel to be unseaworthy, sank it with a torpedo.

In the meantime, at 00.13, the cruiser *Aurora,* from a distance of 7,200 metres, had also focused its fire on the motor vessel *Aspromonte*, on which other units of Force Q also fired until 01.20. In the *Aurora*'s report, it is reported that, proceeding "*on course 045°, speed 25 knots*", the cruiser fired on a merchant ship, of about 2,000 tons, detected by port bow radar, at a distance of 7,800 yards (7,132 metres). The characteristics of the ferry were

▲ The British destroyer *Quentin*. The image is from 1942.
▼ The cruiser *Sirius*, which together with the destroyers *Quiberon* and *Quentin*, subjected the destroyer *Da Recco* to violent artillery fire.

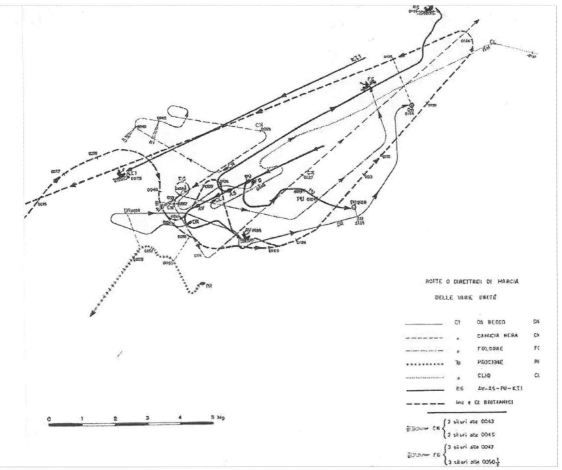

ROTTE O DIRETTRICI DI MARCIA
DELLE VARIE UNITÀ

▲ Outflanking manoeuvre and destruction of convoy H by Q Force (dashed course British cruisers and destroyers). Map Navy Historical Office. The attack manoeuvre of the *Camicia Nera* destroyer is not exact, as the movements of all Italian ships are confused.

▼ The destroyer *Nicoloso da Recco*, which, after being attacked with torpedoes by the destroyer *Camicia Nera*, was targeted by the artillery of the British Q Force units, which hit it with three shells, seriously damaging it.

recognised for its tank landing gear, and it was noted that it had many cargo masts and two medium-calibre guns at the stern. The same ship was later attacked by other British units between 00.13 and 01.20.

The *Aspromonte* (Lieutenant Gaetano Zolese), of 976 gt, was a ferry in the Straits of Messina that had been militarised and armed with military personnel. After colliding with the motor vessel *Puccini and coming to a* halt, it had started up again and reversed course, as per the order received at the start of the fight from the commander of the escort, heading west-northwest at a maximum speed of 16 knots. The *Aspromonte* maintained its undisturbed course until 01:10 when two torpedoes were sighted, which she dodged with the manoeuvre. It is not known that British units had launched the torpedoes at that hour, which Commander Zolese believed to have come from torpedo bombers, which did not exist at all. A quiet ten minutes passed and then, starting at 01.20 and until 01.30, the motor ship was taken under fire by the enemy units, avoiding being hit by the first seven salvoes with the manoeuvre. But then, artillery shells began to hit, starting on the bridge, killing or seriously wounding all the men on it. The commander, who had sustained a flesh wound on his back, took to the helm wheel himself and continued manoeuvring the ship in a zig-zag manner until the helm was hit and immobilised. The attempt to manoeuvre with the engines was unsuccessful, because at 01.29 a.m. a huge explosion occurred on the *Aspromonte*, causing it to sink, with the ship disappearing over the stern. With it was lost its cargo, which included twelve 88 mm cannons, two trucks and forty-nine tons of various materials.

Meanwhile, at 00:21 a.m., the Q Force cruisers had restored speed to 27 knots and targeted the torpedo boat *Clio*, mistaking it for the destroyer *Folgore*, and the British mistakenly believed they had hit it and seen it blow up, when in fact the shots from the British units, first with short salvoes then centred, fell along the sides of the unit, hitting it with shrapnel that did not impair its efficiency. The *Clio, which could* not see the enemy ships because of its smoke, suspended the curtain and returned fire from a distance of 4,500 metres, and suspended it after four salvoes with the two stern pieces, when the enemy unit, which was the cruiser *Argonaut*, on which the Italian torpedo boat was firing, in turn ceased firing with illuminating shells.

The commander of the cruiser *Argonaut*, Captain Langley-Cook, praised the behaviour of the *Clio*, which he mistakenly believed to be the destroyer *Folgore*, writing in his report:

"*Preeminently valiant was the conduct of the last surviving CT, which from about 01.20 onwards, despite being under fire from three cruisers continued to fire at the Argonaut. This CT appears to have been the FOLGORE, which was the only destroyer sunk'*.

As Force Q was pulling to the left to return to Bona, passing north of the Italian ships, the last shots were fired by the cruiser *Sirius at a* presumed destroyer that appeared at 01.26 on the port bow, and ended at 01.35 when the same *Sirius* with the *Quiberon* and *Quentin* conducted concentrated fire on the destroyer *Da Recco*, from a distance of 3,000 metres.

Commander Cocchia, after the appearance of the first artillery flashes from the British ships had put his stern on the enemy and sent the single-word signal 'Combat' into the air, increasing the speed of the destroyer *Da Recco*, ordered all units to go on the attack. At the same time, he opened illuminating fire to detect enemy units. However, he was framed on both sides by artillery salvoes, to which he responded, initiating a firing action that lasted for a few minutes, only to turn to the east when he realised that the enemy had passed astern of him. His manoeuvre to re-engage the British ships and resume the fight was realised when, heading north-east (course 60°), at about 01.30, the Q Force, already on its way back, appeared to him at about 4,000 metres distance three darkened silhouettes which Commander Cocchia believed to be cruisers, intent on firing very intensely at a fourth silhouette which in turn was responding with some liveliness to the fire that was directed against it.

The four ships were at a short distance from each other, and the bright tangs of artillery shells could be clearly seen from the *Da Recco* tiling over the sea on both sides; a close artillery duel that was also seen by the destroyer *Camicia Nera, which was* located far to the east of the *Da Recco,* and which signalled that it was following the same course. During those hours, from 01:20 until 01:30, the fire of the Q Force units was concentrated against the ferry boat *Aventino* which, repeatedly hit, exploded, but there is no record of an exchange of artillery fire with it. We must therefore assume that it was the torpedo boat *Clio* which responded to the enemy fire by firing its two stern guns four salvoes and then disengaged.

Commander Cocchia ordered to put the bow on the three very visible silhouettes of the enemy cruisers while at the same time giving the go-ahead to launch the torpedoes, marking the aiming angle on the 'Paneray'. Next to the commander, in front of the open central hatch of the bridge was Lieutenant Alfredo Zambrini, who assisted in the preparation for the launch. But the order was late in coming because Cocchia, wanting the torpedoes to hit the target for sure, intended to get as close as possible to the target. At this point, according to Cocchia's version, the British units, which as mentioned were the *Sirius*, the *Quiberon* and the *Quentin*, seeing flames coming out of the *Da Recco*'s forward funnel due to the combustion of naphtha residues in the smoke system (sighting of flames not confirmed in the British reports), illuminated the destroyer with illuminating shells and immediately afterwards opened a deadly and intense fire with their cannons. The enemy salvoes enveloped the *Da Recco*, hitting it with three shells, two in the forecastle and one on the hull 1 metre above the waterline, causing, due to the deflagration of charges from an ammunition depot, severe damage that forced the destroyer to stop.

Fortunately, the British ships did not stop their westward course to give the destroyer the coup de grace and, as they moved away, they left the *Da Recco* in flames (with the bow section entirely red-hot including the bridge), full of wounded and burned and immobilised 60 miles by 249° from Marettimo. After giving the necessary orders to save the ship, Commander Cocchia, burned in the face and blinded, handed over command to his second in command, Lieutenant Commander Pietro Riva, who at dawn was able to resume navigation, albeit at reduced speed, towards Trapani, accompanied by the destroyers *Lampo, Pigafetta* and *Da Noli* and the torpedo boat *Partenope* sent to the rescue.

According to the Italian documentation, the steamer *K.T. 1* sank at about 00.40; the *Aventino* at about 00.55; the *Puccini*, which was considered non towable, was immobilized at 01.08 and then sunk at 15.00 by the destroyer *Camicia Nera*; the destroyer *Folgore* sank at 01.16 and the *Aspromonte* at 01.29. Also damaged were the *torpedo* boat *Procione* at 00.53 and the destroyer *Da Recco* at 01.35, while the destroyer *Camicia Nera* and the torpedo boat *Clio* were unharmed.

▲ ► Part of the damage on deck on the left side of the CT *Da Recco*.

▼ Destroyer *Da Recco*. 2 December 1942.

THE RESCUE OF THE CASTAWAYS OF CONVOY H

When Supermarina was informed by the destroyer *Da Recco* that convoy H had been sighted, shortly after 8 p.m. on 1 December, and tailed by British reconnaissance planes, believing that there would be attacks from the enemy, as a precautionary measure it had ordered the hospital ship *Capri*, which set sail from Trapani at 1.40 p.m., to follow the convoy, and a tugboat to stand by at Marettimo. At the same time, the operational body of the Naval High Command had ordered the departure from Palermo of the hospital ship *Laurana*, which left the Sicilian port at 10.30 p.m., delayed due to a fog in the port itself during an air raid warning, also because it had to wait for the fog to clear before moving.

Having received the message '*steamers on fire*' from the *Da Recco* at 01.15 on 2 December, Supermarina ordered the immediate departure from Trapani of the destroyers *Antonio Pigafetta* and *Antonio Da Noli* to the area of the naval collision. The two destroyers left the port at 06.00, to head to the area of the night disaster, and once they reached the waters of Banco Skerki, they participated in the search for the shipwrecked along with the destroyers *Camicia Nera* and *Lampo*, the torpedo boats *Partenope* and *Perseo*, the torpedo boat of the 3rd Squadron *Ms 32*, which with *Ms 31* (Lieutenant Commander Ugo de Grenet) was near Galite Island, and the *Mas 563* and *576*.

▲ Another picture of the damage to the destroyer *Da Recco*.

▼ The *Da Recco* ravaged by flames receives rescue from two destroyers.

▲ Part of the deck damage suffered by the destroyer *Da Recco*.

▼ Destroyer *Da Recco*. Damage on 2 December 1942.

▲ The destroyer *Antonio Da Noli*, who, together with his twin *Antonio Pigafetta*, left Trapani to go to the area of the naval clash to rescue the shipwrecked ships of the H convoy.

▼ Above: the destroyer *Antonio Pigafetta*. Below: the condition of the motor vessel *Puccini* on the morning of 2 December 1942.

▲ The destroyer *Lampo*, which was part of convoy G and came to the rescue of the destroyed convoy H. Above: the *Lampo* at La Spezia in 1936. Below: camouflaged, in the winter of 1942-1943.

▼ The hospital ship (or rescue ship) *Capri* when it was still a transport ship for civil use.

▲ The destroyer *Da Recco*, still operational in Taranto in 1951.

▼ Destroyer *Da Recco*. Damage on 2 December 1942.

The *Lampo* (Lieutenant Commander Antonio Cazzaniti), following the urgent distress signal from the *Da Noli*, had left the escort of the damaged tanker *Giorgio*, of convoy G, which as we know had been torpedoed off the starboard bow by an Albacore aircraft at 21.57 hrs. on 1 December.57 on 1 December, after which the *Giorgio* was left to protect, along with two Mas, the torpedo boat *Climene* (Lieutenant Mario Colussi), and the torpedo boat *Clio*, which at 06.15 had met the tanker after moving away from the burning ships of convoy H. The *Climene,* which was towing the tanker in a slow and laborious navigation towards Trapani, was then replaced by the tug *Liguria* from Taranto, which brought the *Giorgio,* unable to reach Trapani, to run aground at Punta Troia di Marettimo, saving the ship and its precious cargo. The tanker was subsequently beached and taken to Palermo.

In addition to providing for the rescue, Italian and German air reconnaissance had been in action since dawn, whose purpose was to patrol the area where the shipwrecked vessels were located, and to avoid surprises, from the return of enemy naval units, during the rescue operation, and to recover the damaged vessels, the *Da Recco* and the *torpedo* boat *Procione.*

First to come to the rescue of the *Da Recco* was the *Camicia Nera (Camicia Nera),* which had left the combat area on a NE course and at 03.15 had reversed course to give assistance to the survivors, alerting Supermarina. Shortly after dawn, having spotted white smoke and guided by a reconnaissance plane, he reached the area where the survivors of the steamer *Aspromonte were*, on lifeboats and rafts. While he was embarking those men, the *Lampo* arrived, to which the commander of the *Camicia Nera*, frigate captain Adriano Foscari, ordered them to go to the *Da Noli* and report back. Once the recovery of the shipwrecked people from the *Aspromonte was* completed, the Camicia *Nera went to the* motor ship *Puccini*, took aboard the thirty-one men on board and other shipwrecked people at sea nearby. In total, the *Camicia Nera* was able to rescue one hundred and fifty-eight people, four of whom died on board the destroyer.

Subsequently, with the arrival of the *Pigafetta* (sea captain Rodolfo Del Minio) and the *Da Noli* (frigate captain Pio Valdambrini), and considering the *Lampo* and the *Camicia Nera,* four destroyers gathered around the damaged *Da Recco.* The *Camicia Nera* handed over command of the rescue operations to the *Pigafetta,* who immediately took charge of the stern tow of the *Da Recco*, and arranged for the *Lampo to* take on board the wounded, who were then all reunited on the *Da Noli* on which the doctor of the 1t Destroyer Flotilla, to which *Pigafetta* himself belonged as command ship, was stationed. Subsequently, the *Da Noli was* ordered to tranship the wounded onto the hospital ship *Capri* (Lieutenant Oscar Sacchi).

At 09.50 the trailer to the *Da Recco* was ready, and the *Pigafetta*, starting to pull, headed for Trapani where it arrived at 18.00, escorted by the *Lampo*, which had its echo-sounding gear on to search for possible submarines, and the two Mas *563* and *576.* In the meantime, the torpedo boats *Partenope* (Lieutenant Commander Gustavo Lovatelli) and *Perseo* (Lieutenant Severio Marotta) had also arrived in the area of the clash, which, as we know, had been at sea since the night of 1 December on an anti-submarine rake on the

Trapani-Biserta route. Lovatelli, commander of the section, having spotted flashes of a fight in the distance and intercepted a message in which the *Da Recco* communicated that it was in trouble, had warned Marina Trapani that he had suspended the rake to go to the rescue of the destroyer, in whose area, in searches that lasted from 09.10 until 14.00 on 2 December, they rescued numerous shipwrecked people. The *Partenope* rescued 10 shipwrecked from the steamer *Aventino* and 112 others, including 100 from the destroyer *Folgore*; the *Perseo* rescued 150 survivors from the *Aventino*, which she transferred to the hospital ship *Capri*. A further 10 men from the *Aventino* were picked up by the destroyer *Da Noli* and a few more by the motor torpedo boat *Ms 32*.

Having received the order from the *Da Noli* to continue the search until the morning of the following day, the *Capri,* with the assistance of reconnaissance aircraft, was able to rescue another 133 men during the day of 2 December, all belonging to the *Aventino* and the motor-ship Puccini, but needing to get the 14 most seriously wounded to Trapani, it asked the *Ms 32* to pull up to the hospital ship, take the men on board and reach port at maximum speed. Thus, laden with shipwrecked men from the *Da Noli* and the *Perseo,* the *Capri* entered Trapani in the early morning hours of the 3rd, having completed its mission. All the other ships that had participated in the rescue operation had previously reached that port.

The human casualties of the ships of the 'Aventino' convoy, among the nine steamers and escort units, were particularly heavy. Out of a total of 3,300 persons on board, as many as 2,200 were lost. In terms of human lives, the disaster was even greater than the tragic disaster of the convoy 'Duisburg' on 9 November 1941, in the Ionian Sea south of Calabria. Among the 220 casualties, the military units lost 286, as follows: *Da Recco* 118; *Folgore* 124; *Procione* 3; *Aspromonte* 41, i.e. more than a third of the men of these units were lost.

Captain Cocchia of the *Da Recco* and Captain Foscari of the *Camicia Nera* were decorated with the Gold Medal for Military Valour for their valour and, in Memory, Lieutenant Commander Ener Bettica of the sunken destroyer *Freccia* and Lieutenant Alfredo Zambrini of the destroyer *Da Recco*.

BRITISH CONSIDERATIONS

No damage, not even shrapnel, was reported by the British units, who once again, with radar or without radar, proved themselves masters of night combat tactics, both with gun and torpedo. Pleased, perhaps even cynically, at the annihilation of convoy H, by the ships of Force Q, Captain Henry Taprell (Traffaill) Dorling, at the time of the events a kind of Chief Press Officer of the Mediterranean Fleet Command, wrote in his book *Western Mediterranean 1942 - 1945*, translated by the Navy Historical Office

'For the enemy it was a disaster; suddenly engaged at close range, they suffered the loss of four merchant ships and three destroyers all sunk or set on fire. Eyewitnesses told of the destructive effect of the fire at close range, of ships leaping into the air and burning amid clouds of smoke and steam, of trucks carried on deck by the ships rolling overboard as the ships capsized; of terrified men throwing themselves overboard as the ships sank. It is impossible to say how many men the enemy lost, or the number of trucks and the amount of petrol and supplies that failed to reach Tunisia on this occasion. Not a single ship was saved. Some submarines that were in the area the next morning reported that large stretches of sea were covered with a thick layer of naphtha, masses of floating wreckage and a large number of floating corpses with life jackets on. ... Admiral Harcourt reported after the action, 'I think we gave good help to the First Army.

Rear Admiral Harcourt was referring to the British Army of General K.A.N. Anderson fighting in Tunisia. The exact same words written by Traffaill are to be found on p. 377 - 378 of Admiral Andrew Browne Cunningham's book *The Odyssey of a Sailor*, translated by Aldo Fraccaroli for Mondadori publishers.

▲ The destroyers Arrow, Dart and Strale anchored in Genoa harbor in 1938.

A LESSON IN STRATEGY

As I wrote in my book for the Naval Historical Office *Operation Gaudo and the Night Battle of Cape Matapan*, generating much disbelief and surprise at the time (1998), in the British Navy, like the Italian Navy, there was an obligation, especially on nights of poor visibility, for cruiser divisions to be followed by escort destroyers. Force Q departed Bona in the formation described, *Orion, Sirius, Argonaut, Quentin, Quiberon*, attacked the "*Aventino*" convoy and returned to Bona, then departed in the afternoon for Algiers, always proceeding with the cruisers in the lead and the destroyers following, maintaining alignment, as far as possible, even during the night encounter.

I remember that for years it was always said that the Matapan disaster of 28 March 1941 was to be blamed on poor Vice Admiral Carlo Cattaneo, Commander of the 1st Naval Division, because he had kept the destroyers behind the cruisers, depriving himself of an advanced protective screen. None of the admirals and unit commanders, who were familiar with squadron regulations, defended him. On the contrary, the most controversial was the former commander of the Naval Squadron, Admiral Angelo Iachino, the one who was really responsible for the Matapan disaster and who shifted much of the blame onto Cattaneo.

Cattaneo, acting on his own initiative, could have sent the destroyers to the front, but he did not do so in order to comply with what were then the '*Squadron Rules*', which I traced and reported in the book *L'operazione Gaudo e lo scontro notturno di Capo Matapan*, published in 1998 by the Ufficio Storico della Marina Militare Poi, after the disastrous experience of Matapan, the Regia Marina's leadership changed the night navigation and combat regulations, with the destroyers arranged from time to time, and according to the situation, on the front and flanks of the cruisers. Instead, in the Royal Navy, still believing that in melee actions it was the cruisers that should hold the lead in the formation, in order to have a better chance of detecting targets and not to be hampered during firing by their own destroyers which, manoeuvring from the bow, could be mistaken for enemy units, the night navigation rules were maintained by the Royal Navy, with great profit.

I recall that even in the destruction of the convoy 'Beta' ('Duisburg') on the night of 9 November 1941 south of Calabria, Force K's command ship, Captain Agnew's cruiser Aurora, remained at the head of the line of attack during the sailing out of Malta and back, and during the course of the combat.

THE LUFTWAFFE AND REGIA AERONAUTICA COUNTERATTACK

As soon as the attack on the H convoy occurred and the alarm was raised, the OBS and Superaereo ordered the Command of the II Fliegerkorps, in Taormina, and the Command of the Sardinian Air Force, in Cagliari, to intervene immediately with the available units in order to attack the British ships that were returning to base. The order was immediately implemented by sending combat formations into the air. Therefore, in the early hours of the morning, i.e. at 03.15, sixteen torpedo bombers of the 26th Wing (pilot colonel Karl Stockmann) took off from the Sardinian airports, of which twelve He. 111 of Group I./ KG.26 and four Ju. 88s of Group III./KG.26, respectively commanded by Major Pilot Werner Klümper and Horst Kayser.

The torpedo bombers were shortly followed, with takeoff from Sicily taking place between 04:37 and 04:47, by thirteen Ju. 88 bombers of the 54th Wing (Lieutenant Colonel Pilot Walter Marienfeld) divided into three formations of three, four and six aircraft, respectively of Groups I./KG.54, II./KG.54 and III./KG.54. The first to sight the ships of a British convoy were the torpedo bombers of KG.26, but only a few of them, due to bad weather encountered along the route, carried out the attack.

OBS bulletin No. 371 of 4 December states: '*sank a probably British escort ship 'PC 74' and attacked a cruiser with effect not observed due to fog: most convoy aircraft not found due to bad weather'.*

From the above, it can be deduced that the alleged escort ship 'PC 74' was hardly the destroyer *Quentin*, whose sinking (prior to my research in the 1970s) had been credited to Italian or German torpedo bombers. Instead, at that time the Force Q was distant from the convoy, as it was moving from the Sicilian Channel on a westerly course south of Galite Island.

At 06.36 the *Quentin* (Lieutenant Commander Allen Herbert Percy Noble) was attacked by three Ju. 88 aircraft of I./KG.54 (Lieutenant Colonel Pilot Helmut von Raven), and the German crews, as reported in OBS Bulletin No. 370 of December 3, 1942, reported that a 500 kilogram bomb had hit the side of a destroyer, arresting it. The Ju. 88's action took place at low altitude at 06.40 hours (time given in the OBS report) at lat. 37°27'N, long. 08°35'E, corresponding to 36 miles north of Tabarka, near Tunisia's border with Algeria. As the attack unfolded in the uncertain pre-dawn light, made even gloomier by the bad weather, the bomb that struck the *Quentin*'s starboard side, about 8 feet (about 2.5 metres) from the engine room bulkhead, gave the British the impression that the destroyer had been hit by a torpedo, not least because the attacking aircraft arrived by surprise and was not sighted.

The condition of the stricken ship (due to immediate flooding of the boiler room and other rooms in the vicinity, the knocking out of the pumping system, the removal of a quadruple set of torpedoes thrown overboard, and the collapse of the right platform of the

▲ The sloop *PC 74*, which the German torpedo bomber crews of I. and III./KG.26 on the morning of 2 December re-tried to hit and sunk in convoy, north of Bona.

▲ A formation of Ju. 88's from the 6ᵗʰ Squadron of the 54ᵗʰ Bomb Wing (6./KG.54) of the II Fliegerkorps taken off in formation from an airfield in Italy in 1942. Note the large anti-ship bomb under the nacelle of the aircraft.

▼ Officers of KG.54 (KampfGeschwader 54) at a Stormo aircraft, whose emblem was the skull.

▲ Picture of a Ju.88 from I./KG.54.

Oerlikon gunboat) immediately appeared desperate, and the crew (182 men including the commander and 7 officers) were rescued by the destroyer *Quiberon* (frigate captain Hugh Waters Shelley Browning), under the onslaught of the Ju. 88 which caused some damage to the latter ship, due to a bomb that fell near the hull.

After the *Quentin* had been hit and arrested, abandoned by the *Quiberon* in position lat. 37°32'N, long. 08°32'E (corresponding to 54 miles by 48° from Cap de Garde), to join, at a speed of 33 knots, the Q Force cruisers that were moving away, the succession of attacks, again referring to the daily German operational bulletins, was as follows.

They first attacked the four Ju. 88s of II./KG.54 (Major Richard Taubert), which dropped on the *Quentin,* which appeared to be stationary and with its stern under water, and hit it amidships on the port side with another 500-pound bomb, which the British once again mistook for a second torpedo. The destroyer seemed to break into two pieces. There was a violent explosion, following which the *Quentin* sank rapidly astern in about fifteen seconds, twenty minutes after being abandoned by the *Quiberon*.

This was reported by a Board of Inquiry set up after the return of Force Q to Bona, which severely judged the actions of Commander Browning, of the *Quiberon*, for hastily and negligently abandoning the *Quentin* before finishing her off with the torpedo, since important documents of the ship, had the destroyer remained afloat, might have fallen into enemy hands. But it must be considered, in Browning's defence, that he stayed with the *Quentin* for about ten minutes, and that if he had torpedoed the damaged destroyer while crewmen were still on board looking for documents and personal effects, there would have been many casualties.

▲ Captain Cimicchi, first from the left, looks at the propeller of a torpedo together with Captain Buscaglia. The picture was taken in Rhodes in 1941 when Cimicchi was serving in the 281st A.S. Squadron and Buscaglia was its commander.

Finally, the third formation of Ju. 88s arrived, made up of six aircraft of III./KG.54 (pilot captain Hermann Donandt), three of which dropped their bombs against the destroyer *Quiberon*, which was seen to stop leaving behind large oil stains, while the other three Ju 88s, having failed to track the Q Force, continued on to Bona, Tabarca and La Calle to attack, as a secondary target, port depots.[36]

Twenty men were missing from the *Quentin*'s crew, but nine of them were rescued at 12 noon on that 2 December by a German Do. 24 seaplane of the 3rd Rescue Squadron based in Syracuse, and were taken prisoner.[37]

---

36 At 08.25 a.m. on December 2, 1942, the Liaison Office of the Regia Aeronautica at the O.B.S. telephoned Superaereo to report that a German bomber had reported: "*06.43 enemy unit on course and speed unspecified at 37°12'N, 08°15'E*". This was evidently the destroyer *Quiberon*, which, having abandoned the sinking sectional unit *Quentin* was maneuvering to rejoin the cruisers of Force Q, and which at that hour was attacked and damaged by the Ju. 88s of III./KG.54. With a subsequent telephone call at 15.50 hours, the Regia Aeronautica Liaison Office at O.B.S. informed Superaereo "*that at 37°07' - 8°45'*" a destroyer had "*been seen sinking - Said destroyer would be sunk by the II C.A.T.*". Naturally, it could only be the *Quentin*.

37 Colonel La Latta, of the Office of the Regia Aeronautica at the O.B.S., in a letter about the activity of the 2nd Luftflotte, with the subject "*Actions against enemy operations in the Western Mediterranean during day 2 and night on 3/12/1942*", among other things wrote: "*35 aircraft employed for the attack against enemy formation of light naval forces returning to Bona [Forza Q]. Due to poor weather conditions only 10 aircraft found naval targets, which were attacked in poor visibility conditions. A C.T. and an escort ship were sunk. The result of the other attacks against CC.TT. and 1 light cruiser could not be observed. 3 aircraft attacked as secondary targets Bona, Tabarca and La Calle. Observed in Bona hits on warehouses with consequent development of smoke'*.

According to Italian reports from Sardinia Air Force Command, transmitted to Superaereo, at 08.55 hrs, i.e. when the *Quentin had* already been hit and sunk for over two hours by the Ju.88 bombers of I./KG.54 and II./KG.54, on orders from the Sardinian Air Force Command, eight S. 79 torpedo bombers of the 130th Group took off from Elmas to track down and attack the Q Force: five of the 283rd Squadron led by Major Pilot Franco Menley; and three of the 280th Squadron commanded by Captain Pilot Giuseppe Cimicchi.

En route to the Galite Islands area, Major Melley's S.79 suffered engine trouble and had to return to base. The remaining seven aircraft, navigating in single formation, on their way towards the British ships at 09.50 sighted a convoy north of Cape Serrat, east of Tabarca. By this time, Q Force was no longer at sea, having entered the port of Bona at 09.43 on 2 December, and in the meantime it had not reported any other air attack after the one that led to the sinking of the *Quentin*. Force Q left in the afternoon for Algiers, as the port of Bona was subjected to heavy bombardment by German and Italian aircraft in those days, which had resulted in losses and damage to ships.

As they were beginning their attack manoeuvre, the torpedo bombers were intercepted by three RAF Spitfires which, being escorting the convoy, mistakenly mistook the S. 79s for Breda 88 aircraft. They first attacked Lieutenants Homblin and Lindsay, of the 242nd Squadron, and then Lieutenant Colonel Petrus Hendrik Hugo, commander of the 322nd Wing. The result was flattering for the British pilots, who managed to shoot down no less than four Italian torpedo bombers, one of them after dropping the torpedo. These were the S. 79s of Lieutenants Manlio Caresio and Ferruccio Loprieno and Second Lieutenants Antonio Vellere and Amorino Ingrosso. The crew of the Ceresio, on which the chosen marconist airman Aldo Manca had died, and two other airmen had suffered minor injuries, was rescued, after a good fifty-five hours, by a German Do. 24 seaplane of the 3rd Flottiglia Soccorso and taken to the Stagnone seaplane station.

The remaining three S.79s, led by Captain Cimicchi, retreated after also dropping torpedoes, and the crews, having returned to base, optimistically reported that they had hit a cruiser and a steamer, and shot down a Spitfire.[384] On the British side, hit by the machine-gunners of Lieutenant Caresio's S.79, Lieutenant Hamblin's Spitfire plunged into flames. The officer jumped with his parachute, ending up in the sea but was never found.

---

38 On the attack of the three torpedo bombers, General Carlo Unia, author of *Storia degli Aerosiluranti Italiani (History of Italian Torpedo Planes),* reported in a very schematic manner: '*Lt. Cimicchi and the two surviving wingmen managed to launch their torpedoes and believed they had hit an incr. and a steamer.* Instead, in the Diario Storico dell'Aviazione della Sardegna it is written: '*The action was not completed because Spitfire aircraft attacked the formation and shot down 4 of our aircraft. One Spitfire was shot down by one of our aircraft*'.

▲ The British CT *Quentin*, which on its way back to Bona, after the attack on the *Aventino* convoy, was hit and sunk by German bombers of I./KG.54 and II./KG.54, of the II Fliegerkorps, around dawn on 2 December, which also damaged the twin *Quiberon*.

▼ The Australian destroyer *Quiberon* photographed in 1942 at sea by an aircraft.

THE FATE OF CONVOY C

The annihilation of convoy H (*Aventino*) and the torpedoing of the only merchant ship of convoy G, the tanker *Giorgio,* which had to be run aground near Trapani, had an equally tragic aftermath with regard to another convoy, C, which had left Naples for Tripoli, and which Supermarina had deemed the least attackable by Force Q, because it was the furthest away, following a route skirting the western coast of Sicily, and then transiting along the eastern coast of Tunisia.

In reality, as we have said, as early as 29 November, the Ultra cryptographic organisation, by deciphering the codes of the German Enigma and Italian C.38 ciphering machines, had reported to the British Admiralty, and from the latter had relayed to Malta, the news that a convoy for Tripoli with the steamers *Chisone* and *Veloce* were to "*set sail from Naples at 9 p.m. on the 30th, their departure having been postponed by 24 hours, speed 9 knots for Tripoli and should arrive at 8.30 p.m. on the 3rd*". This allowed the Malta Command to organise the air-sea interception in the best possible way.

Sighted by Malta's scouts as early as the evening of 1 December between Sicily and Pantelleria, and then again in the waters of the Kerkennah Islands on the evening of the 2nd, it was confirmed that convoy C consisted of two 5,000-tonne merchant ships, and was escorted by a supposed cruiser, a destroyer and a torpedo boat.

In reality, the convoy comprised the motor vessel *Chisone* and the steamer *Veloce*, while the tanker *Devoli*, unmarked by the Ultra organisation, had been included in it as far as Trapani, and then entered that port on the evening of day 1.

Initially escorting the two remaining merchantmen were the torpedo boats *Lupo* (Lieutenant Commander Giuseppe Folli), *Aretusa* (Lieutenant Commander Roberto Guidotti) and *Sagittario* (Lieutenant Lieutenant Vittorio Barich), but the latter had abandoned the convoy on the evening of 1 December due to a breakdown, which had meanwhile been joined by the torpedo boat *Ardente* (Lieutenant Lieutenant Rinaldo Ancillotti).

Following the sighting of the C convoy in Kerkennah waters, at 17.42 nine FAA aircraft took off from Malta in two waves, the first comprising two Albacore of the 828th Squadron, led by an Albacore ASV of the 821st Squadron, which was followed by six more torpedo bomber aircraft of the same unit. Meanwhile, at 14.00 hours, the destroyers of Force K, reconstituted in Malta with the units of the 14th *Jervis* Flotilla (Captain Albert Lawrence Poland), *Janus* and *Javelin*, part of Admiral Henry Harwood's Mediterranean Fleet, with headquarters in Alexandria, had sailed from Valletta.

Convoy C was sighted by the first wave aircraft at 7.30 p.m. on 2 December, lat. 34°45' N, long. 11°45' E, and immediately attacked by the three Albacores of pilot Lieutenants Taylor and Simpson, of the 828th Squadron, and Graham of the 821st. It was undoubtedly Taylor who scored his torpedo on the 5,464 gt steamer *Veloce*, which sank around 8pm.

▲ An S.79 of the 283rd Aerosilurant Squadron, ready for take-off at Elmas (Cagliari), with the torpedo fixed under the right wing.

▼ An S.79 aircraft of the 280th Squadron of the 130th Aero Group flying over the Mediterranean Sea in search of enemy ships.

▲ A German radio broadcasting station. On the left is the Enigma cipher machine.

▼ Decoders from the Ultra cryptographic organisation at their headquarters in Bletchley Park, north London.

▲ The torpedo boat *Arethusa*, one of the escort units to convoy G, bound for Tunis, which it did not reach because of damage to the tanker *Giorgio*, torpedoed by an Albacore naval aircraft from Malta's 828th Squadron.

▼ Admiral Henry Harwood, Commander of the Mediterranean Fleet, visiting the port of Benghazi captured by the British Army on 20 November 1942, and full of sunken shipwrecks.

▲ The torpedo boat *Ardente*, which together with the torpedo boat *Lupo* escorted convoy C.

▼ The torpedo boat *Lupo* as it crosses the Taranto harbour channel.

▲ Malta, Hal Far British Naval Airfield. In the car park, with its torpedo, ready for take-off an Albacore aircraft of the 828th Squadron.

▼ A section of three Albacore torpedo bombers of the 828th Squadron took off from Malta to attack Italian ships in the central Mediterranean.

▲ The Italian steamer *Chisone*, one of the two merchant ships of convoy C bound for Tripoli, which managed to escape the attack of the Albacore torpedo bombers.

▼ The British destroyer *Jervis* commanded the 14th Squadron of the Mediterranean Fleet, which exercised command of Force K in Malta. With three other units it attacked convoy G in the Sicilian Channel, sinking the torpedo boat *Lupo*.

▲ The Italian steamer Veloce (when it was called *Media*), which, together with the torpedo boat *Lupo* was sunk by British destroyers of Force K, sailed from Malta.

▲ Captain Albert Lawrence Poland, Commander of the 14th Destroyer Flotilla.

The steamer *Chisone*, escorted by the torpedo boats *Aretusa* and *Ardente*, continued on her way to Tripoli, having escaped Graham's attack, as Simpson fired at the alleged cruiser, optimistically claiming that he had hit it and set it alight.

The torpedo boat *Lupo,* which had stayed behind to rescue the *Veloce*, while it was engaged in recovering the shipwrecked steamer was sighted at midnight by the destroyers of Force K, which were proceeding in a line of lines, and which were directed towards the target by the tracers of anti-aircraft fire upwards from the Italian ships, and by the flashes of a burning ship, the *Veloce* not yet sunk.

Using radar to their advantage, which the Italian ships escorting convoy C did not have, the British destroyers, reducing their speed, silently reached a distance of 2,000 yards (1,828 metres) from the *Lupo*, when flotilla leader *Jervis* began firing, having illuminated the target with his 40-inch searchlight. The first salvo demolished the torpedo boat's deck, the second salvo immobilised the engine room. Then, still holding his searchlight on the *Lupo, he* brought his ships in a semicircle around the immobilised torpedo boat. Cynically, before resuming his course for Malta, without worrying about the shipwrecked crewmen, Captain Poland began a relentless pounding on the small craft, and a series of broadsides, fired from twenty-four 120 mm cannons, literally demolished her. At the same time, still using artillery, the units of Force K, before moving away, delivered the coup de grace to the steamer *Veloce*.

The torpedo boat *Ardente*, which had left the escort to the steamer *Chisone*, returned and picked up the survivors of the *Lupo* (29 men) and the *Veloce*, taking them to Trapani where it arrived on the morning of 4 December.

Also on 2 December, at 18.30 in the afternoon, the British submarine *Umbra* (P 35), under the command of Lieutenant Stephen Lynch Conwway Maydon, had attacked and sunk the isolated 1,097 gt Italian steamer *Sacro Cuore*, 15 miles east of Mahadia, at the southern end of the Gulf of Hammamet. The crew of the steamer, who together with ten German air force personnel had taken places on a rescue boat, were left free to reach the coast of Tunisia. Instead, the ten Germans were captured, boarded on the submarine and taken to Malta.

▲ The Italian steamer *Sacro Cuore*, when it was called *Gwynwood*. It was sunk by the *Umbra* on 2 December 1942.

▲ The turret of the submarine *Umbra* (P 35) with crewmen celebrating victories on war missions.

▼ In the famous picture of 3 June 1941 taken by an Italian aircraft, the arrival in Taranto of the torpedo boat *Lupo*, which had been damaged north of Crete in the night-time clash of 21 May with British units of Force D of the Mediterranean Fleet. Note the crew lined up for the salute and the bullet holes that had hit the ship's hull.

CONCLUSIONS

In Supermarina's letter, transmitted on 17 March 1943 to Maristat, the following and most interesting remarks on the tactics employed by the British naval forces against the 'Aventino' convoy were made by Rear Admiral Lorenzo Gasparri, to be imitated during night naval combat:[39]

"From what could be detected, the enemy made extensive but generally rapid and fleeting use of its searchlights. It could be deduced from this that he employed them only as a means of recognising the units he discovered by his optical or electro-magnetic means. It was not noted that he made use of recognition or melee signals, while for his own firing he generally made use of illuminating searchlights and aerial flares.

This use of [window] searchlights as a means of rapid recognition of units sighted at sea, especially in confused situations, seems worthy of examination. The searchlight in fact has the advantages over the recognition and melee signals which we envisage of allowing a quicker and safer recognition and of hindering the sighted unit from using its weapons, thus retaining priority in the offence to itself. On the other hand, it has the disadvantage of being visible at a great distance, but in the event of an abundance of lights and artifices that make the location of the encounters obvious over a wide area.

Once again, the enemy's technical and training superiority in night fights was revealed.

The enemy firing always appeared quick, precise, concentrated and in a very short time brought about initial effects to our Units.

Effective was always his illuminating shot. At close range, the enemy made use of their machine guns with material and moral effects that must not have been slight. Against the AVENTINO and PUCCINI he also seems to have made effective use of torpedoes.

The use of our weapons does not appear to be as effective".

Rear Admiral Gasparri's report highlighted the 'admirable behaviour *in terms of boldness and line of conception*' of the destroyers *Camicia Nera* and *Folgore*; above all, '*most admirable*' was that of the *Folgore*, which sacrificed itself by immediately launching an attack against the enemy even though the operation order had entrusted it with the task of '*staying with the convoy and protecting its rapid evacuation*'. Equally praiseworthy was the initiative of the *Camicia Nera*, who, having spotted the position of the enemy ships by the glow of the shining tails of the bullets they were firing, had directed "*immediately to the attack, without waiting for confirmation from the Escort Chief, emitting a smoke screen to cover the steamers*". Turning then to the behaviour of the commanders of the two destroyers, Lieutenant Commander Erner Bettiga of the *Folgore* and Frigate Captain Adriano Foscari of the *Camicia Nera*, although they had not managed 'to *avoid the destruction of the DA RECCO convoy*', Rear-Admiral Gasparri added: "*Both Commanders demonstrated a decisiveness, an aggres-*

---

39 AUSMM, *Naval Action of 2 December*, Prot. No. 11961 of 17 March 1943.

▲ The destroyer *Camicia Nera* not yet camouflaged.
▼ Twin 'Scotti' machine-gun assemblies on board an Italian torpedo boat in the second half of 1942.

sive spirit, a readiness, a tactical manoeuvring skill that can be described as admirable. It may have lacked in part, due to the well-known deficiency in the preparation and training of our Units for night engagements, technical perfection in the employment of weapons, but the heart and soul were unparalleled.[40]

In going on the attack against a more numerous and stronger enemy, of whose technical and training superiority in night combat the Italian Navy had made repeated and painful experience, the two units were devoted to sacrifice and their Commanders must have known this. In fact, the FOLGORE found in action a heroic and glorious end that was to be expected. The CAMICIA NERA on the other hand, assisted by incredible luck, the luck that helps the daring, had neither a hit nor a wounded".

Regarding the destroyer *Da Recco* (and in particular its commander Captain Aldo Cocchia) Rear Admiral Gasparri was not as enthusiastic, writing:[41]

"He was the Escort Chief Unit. His behaviour is also very praiseworthy, but it does not appear as straight, linear, without flaws as that of the FOLGORE and the CAMICIA NERA.

It can first be noted that its commander did not show excessive initiative. The 150801 signal with which Supermarina ordered the 'Mistral' Group to reinforce the escort of convoy 'Sirius' [convoy B] 'against possible coming from Bona where some cc.tt. were present this morning' was given no importance. On the contrary, the commander thought that Supermarina judged only the convoy furthest behind to be under threat, and that there was therefore no danger to him. He thought the same thing when, shortly before midnight, he received the 2344 discovery signal with which Supermarina communicated the sighting made at 2240 hours by a C.A.T. [German Air Corps - II Fliegerkorps] aircraft of 5 unspecified units, proceeding at high speed towards the east, and when he noted that the MAESTRALE and not the DA RECCO had been asked to receive this signal.

From this last phase, with no comment from Rear Admiral Gasparri, it is clear that Supermarina, in failing to inform *Da Recco* directly, had made an unforgivable mistake. Especially since Force Q was at the time of the aerial sighting some 75 miles from *Da Recco*, whose convoy was therefore the most threatened by the enemy coming from the west. On the other hand, not having directly received the news of the aerial sighting, Commander Cocchia was led to believe that convoy B, which was the strongest (three destroyers and five torpedo boats), would be attacked, and consequently, as Rear-Admiral Gasparri wrote, Captain Cocchia *'militarily tough and stubborn in rigidly following his own orders'*, continued to steer the course (245th) set in the order of operations, and at 0001 on 2 December, in the imminence of the enemy attack, merely requested orders from Supermarina, which did not arrive in time.

When the enemy attack developed, in a particularly favourable situation due to the scattering of the H convoy following the slight collision between the steamers *Puccini* and *Aventino, and the* dispersion of the ships also caused by what were erroneously believed to be air attacks, Commander Coccia found himself in the position of not understanding

---

40 AUSMM, CC.TT. Squadron Command, *Naval Action of 2 December 1942*, Prot. No. 04261/S of 12 March 1943.
41 *Ibid.*

▲ The four fighters of the Navy's 8ᵗʰ Squadron: *Fulmine, Baleno, Lampo* and *Folgore* at their mooring at Punta della Salute in Venice in 1938.

▼ Another image of the CT *Folgore* while manoeuvring at sea.

▲ Another image of the CT *Folgore* at anchor in the harbour.

▼ Always the CT *Folgore* with sheets hanging out to dry (perhaps Brindisi).

which side the British units were on, and was absorbed for some time in giving orders to the escort ships to go on the attack and to cover the merchant ships with fog. Having to justify himself for not having immediately directed against the enemy, in imitation of the manoeuvres of the *Folgore* and the *Camicia Nera*, Commander Cocchia claimed to have directed, in a confused situation also due to the light devices that could be seen in the air, not in the '*presumed' direction of the enemy*, but in the '*exact*' direction of the enemy gunfire, with the result of not arriving in this first phase of the battle in contact with the adversary, whom he was unable to sight in his rush towards the west.

At this point, he decided to change course to the east, in order to catch the enemy from behind, while he was still engaged against the steamers, and in doing so, while he was adjusting his course on the distant flashes of some fires, he signalled to the other ships: "*We are rounding the enemy from the west*". At 01.00 hours, having seen a destroyer on the starboard bow, Commander Cocchia prepared to launch torpedoes, only to immediately give up fearing that it was a national unit, as in fact it was since it was the *Camicia Nera*, which must have already carried out its failed attack against the *Da Recco*. The idea that it was the torpedo boat *Procione* that was sighted, as is written in Rear Admiral Gasparri's report, leaves legitimate doubts, since at that time the torpedo boat, the only Italian ship south of Force Q, passed astern of the *Da Recco*, and not forward, as is shown on the map of the Ufficio Storico della Marina Militare.

As he continued in his pursuit of the enemy, with the situation looking increasingly uncertain, at 00.33 Commander Cocchia spotted the silhouettes of three naval units, which appeared to be firing on the opposite side, and he directed his attack against them. But this initiative was unsuccessful, because the *Da Recco*, before he could deploy his weapons, was caught under fire by the units of the Q Force, which hit him severely, arresting him in flames. Fortunately, having already set course at 01.26 to return to Bona, the enemy did not linger to give the destroyer the coup de grace, and this allowed the *Da Recco* to be rescued and survive.

Commander Cocchia's manoeuvre to seek out the British ships to the north, after '*having shown little initiative in the pre-tactical phase and perhaps little readiness in the first moments of the clash*', was greatly appreciated, and although the manoeuvre did not bring the hoped-for results, the officer, who had been seriously wounded, fully deserved the Gold Medal for Military Valour that was awarded to him on the field, according to Rear Admiral Gasparri.

In the post-war period, Lieutenant Admiral Aldo Cocchia was Director of the Navy's Historical Office, and among his publications are the two first volumes on '*The Defence of Traffic with North Africa*', which are worthy of note in every respect. However, the compilation of the 3rd volume, which deals with the destruction of the convoy '*Aventino*', with all the aftermath that followed, was entrusted to Admiral Giuseppe Fioravanzo.

Regarding the behaviour of the *torpedo* boat *Procione, commanded* by Lieutenant Commander Renato Torchiana, the reports do not contain any significant elements that would have led to an effective offensive action. Not least because, despite being at a distance

▲ The British destroyer *Quentin*. As we have described it was sunk on 2 December 1942 by German Ju. 88 bombers of I. and II./KG.54. It represented the only British loss during the operation that led to the destruction of the '*Aventino*' convoy.

of 2,000 metres from the enemy units, on the commander's order '*out*', the torpedo boat did not fire its torpedoes '*due to the severing of normal electrical and telephone connections*. An anomaly that, according to Rear Admiral Gasparri, the commander of a well-trained ship would have had to overcome somehow. The *Raccoon was* badly hit, but despite her precarious condition she managed to save herself.

Even the behaviour of the torpedo boat *Clio* was not exempt from criticism, for in the event of an attack it should have stayed with the convoy, but instead on the initiative of its commander it went in search of the enemy, and when the *Da Recco*'s 00.38 order came, '*Reverse course immediately. Make fog*', he could no longer find the steamers. And even his firing action with the Australian destroyer *Quiberon*, known after the war, in which he fired four salvoes from a distance of 4,500 metres, was at the time considered irrelevant to the defence of the convoy, indeed Rear-Admiral Gasparri considered it '*entirely negative*'. However, this was also justified by the fact that the torpedo boat did not have its own commanding officer, Lieutenant Ugo Tonani, who had disembarked due to illness and was replaced by Lieutenant Vito Asaro, who in the difficult conditions in which he found himself was not prepared to bear the burdens of that command.

Finally, with regard to the steamers in the convoy, it was noted that they were completely unresponsive with their own cannon, and that only a few magazines had been fired with the anti-aircraft guns.

In conclusion, Force Q was able to make contact with convoy H with great ease, guided by Malta's air reconnaissance, which proved to be highly efficient in providing reports on the movements of Italian ships, and by making adequate use of radar, which, however, did not give a great demonstration of efficiency, so much so that Rear Admiral Harcourt wrote in his report No. 241/E

"It was disappointing that the Type 271 radar did not detect the convoy at a distance of more than 6 miles, but due to the rain showers the screen was providing confusing data".

The British formation, once it sighted the convoy, headed for it from west to east, opening fire at short range and with extraordinary precision. Its action against the steamers was swift and decisive, and initially only the ferryboat *Aspromonte*, increasing its speed to 16 knots, managed to get away, evading the hunt for an hour and twenty minutes, before being sunk.

It was also found that the enemy ships employed their own heavy machine-gun complexes (40 mm four-barrel pom-poms), while the Italian torpedo boats did not, having only the modest twin 20 mm machine-guns available. In addition, the artillery shells of each unit had different coloured light tails (red, green, bluish, yellow), so that in collective firing, it was clear when each individual ship was firing at the same target.

Finally, by holding the line, Force Q avoided having to light the melee lights, thus preventing Italian units from locating the enemy and causing mistakes such as that of the *Camicia Nera* with *Da Recco*.

Despite every effort made by the Regia Marina to try and improve training, the annihilation of the 'Aventino' convoy, with the sinking of four merchant ships and an escort destroyer, to which was added in the Sicilian Channel the loss of part of convoy C bound for Tripoli (a steamer and a torpedo boat), confirmed that the Italian units, after two and a half years of war, were still not sufficiently prepared for night combat.

Even the improvements that were attempted in the following months to overcome the gap that existed with the Royal Navy did not bring the hoped-for successes, and 8 September 1943 found the Regia Marina struggling with training problems, which suffered from a lack of combat equipment suitable for fighting in the dark; Above all, there was a lack of efficient radar equipment (the 'Owl', the only naval-grade radiolocator built by the national industry, was a real disappointment) and optical instruments with great night light; and there was still the almost implausible need for a sufficient number of good binoculars to be assigned for surveillance to the lookouts on individual ships.

▲ ▼ The crew of the Caccia Maestrale (behind the commander Ernesto Basilio Cristini, the editor's uncle). On 30 November, together with the Grecale and the Ascari, he carried out a mine-laying mission in the Sicilian Channel; On his return from this mission, he was sent, with the rest of the 10th Squadron, to reinforce the escort of convoy "B" (from Naples to Tunisia with the steamers Arlesiana, Achille Lauro, Campania, Menes and Lisboa and the original escort of the torpedo boats *Sirius*, Orione, Groppo and Pallade to which another torpedo boat, the Uragano, was later added), which was, however, pulled back on news of the British Force Q, which would later take part in the tragic battle we have recounted.

▲ The crew of an Italian submarine in 1942, possibly the *Lazzaro Mocenigo*.

CHRONOLOGY OF GOLD MEDALS FOR MILITARY VALOUR

Adriano FOSCARI, Frigate Captain

Gold Medal for Military Valour

Commander of a destroyer, escorting a convoy of cargo ships, suddenly attacked by much superior enemy naval forces, he boldly launched himself to the attack, penetrating with his ship between the units of the adversary formation. Discovered by the enemy and subjected to a violent reaction of fire, he did not desist from the daring action he had started, firmly determined to carry it through to the end and inflict as much damage on the adversary as possible, regardless of the continuous thick salvoes that framed his unit. He thus managed to launch his torpedoes at a group of destroyers. Having sighted a cruiser soon after and determined to conduct a second attack, he manoeuvred with great skill under the fire that the enemy concentrated on his ship and, having reached the target, moved to a very close range and hit it with two torpedoes that caused it to explode and sink immediately. Having thus exhausted his torpedoes, he continued to search for the adversary with the intention of attacking him with the cannon and, only after having ascertained that the enemy had finally moved away, did he set out to search for and recover the shipwrecked men, returning to base the following evening. Throughout the action, he demonstrated exceptional qualities as a commander, nourished by a high spirit of initiative and the most tenacious aggressiveness.

Sicily Channel, 2 December 1942.

He was born in Venice on 10 June 1904. A student at the Livorno Naval Academy from 1918, in July 1922 he was appointed Ensign. He had various embarkation destinations and in 1929, in the rank of Lieutenant of Vascello, he took up the post of Officer of Ordnance to HRH the Duke of Aosta and from 1930 to October 1933 he was Officer Attaché to the Military House of the Duke of Spoleto. In 1934 he had the command of the torpedo boat 75 OLT, then that of the torpedo boat Acerbi and finally that of the submarine Des Geneys. Promoted to Lieutenant Commander in May 1936 and assigned to the Maritime Warfare Institute, in March 1938 he was in command of the submarine Sciesa and then the submarine Veniero. In August 1939 he was appointed Chief of the General Staff Secretariat at the Ministry of the Navy and in January 1940 he was promoted to Frigate Captain. In January 1942, he was given command of the destroyer Camicia Nera, with which he carried out numerous convoy escort missions. On a mission to escort a convoy of cargo ships to a port in Libya, he was suddenly attacked on the night of 2 December by overwhelming enemy naval forces near the Skerki Bank, on the Tunisian coast, and he daringly brought his unit to the attack, penetrating inside the enemy formation. Although under heavy fire, he managed to launch his torpedoes at a group of enemy destroyers. He then sighted a cruiser, went on the attack again and with the precise firing of two torpedoes he sank it. When the torpedoes were exhausted, he continued the fight with the on-board guns, forcing the enemy, hit by his salvoes, to turn away. For this action he was mentioned in the War Bulletin.

He took part in the war of liberation, first as a liaison officer with the Supreme Command and then as Commander of the 'San Marco' Regiment, a command he held until the end of hostilities. Placed in auxiliary status on request in February 1947 and enrolled in the reserve, he was promoted to Rear Admiral. Rear Admiral Adriano Foscari died in Venice on 22 June 1980.

Other decorations:

Bronze Medal for Military Valour in the Field (Central Mediterranean, January 1942);

Bronze Medal for Military Valour in the Field (Ionian Sea, August 1942);

Military Cross for Valour in the Field (Western Mediterranean, June 1942);

Knight of the Military Order of Italy (1944-1945).

Aldo COCCHIA, Captain of Vessel

Gold Medal for Military Valour

Commander of a Destroyer and Chief of Escort of a convoy that, at night, was crossing a strongly threatened sea area, he became aware of the approach of enemy naval units that were overwhelming in number, tonnage and technical means, and immediately launched himself and his dependent units to attack, also arranging for the protection of the convoy's ships. Promptly appreciating the situation, he began a daring manoeuvre to outflank the adversary, carrying out three separate firing actions in an attempt to engage him, distract his fire from the convoy's units and be able to beat him from a position favourable to torpedo firing. During the third firing action, some enemy salvoes hit his unit, arresting it and causing a violent fire inside and outside the forward ammunition depot, the blaze of which severely burned and charred almost everyone on the bridge. Although physically maimed by the very serious burns to his head and hands, he maintained command of his ship for

over two hours, carrying out effective action to attempt his rescue. Even when his physical condition, preventing him from using his eyesight, forced him to hand over command to his second in command, he maintained command of the rescue operation, with a high sense of responsibility and stoic disregard for the atrocious suffering, managing to keep his ship afloat, which would otherwise have been lost with its crew.

Skerki Bank (Sicilian Channel), night on 2 December 1942

He was born in Naples on 30 August 1900. After leaving the Livorno Naval Academy, not yet 17 years old, with the rank of Ensign, he took part in the First World War embarked on the battleship Conte di Cavour. In subsequent ranks he had boarding assignments and command of MAS, submarines and surface torpedo boats and took part in military operations during the Italian-Ethiopian conflict and in the Spanish Civil War. During the Second World War he had command of the submarine Torelli in the Atlantic, was Chief of Staff of Betasom in Bordeaux and later Commander of the Italian Naval Expedition that occupied the eastern part of the island of Crete in 1941. In early January 1942, he assumed command of the XVI Destroyer

Squadron with the da Recco insignia, ensuring the defence of numerous convoys bound for North Africa. In December 1942, during a convoy escort mission, he sustained, on the night of the 2ⁿᵈ, a hard naval combat against overwhelming enemy forces, launching himself to the attack and at the same time preparing the defence of the convoy. When his unit was hit by a few enemy salvoes, immobilised and with a heavy fire on board, he suffered very serious injuries due to the burns he had sustained, but even when his physical condition, aggravated by the momentary loss of sight that forced him to pass command to his second in command and prevented him from moving, he kept the direction of the rescue operations, managing to keep the ship afloat. The very serious wounds he sustained in the action forced him into a long hospital stay, which lasted over three years. Transferred to the Role of Honour, in which he attained the rank of Lieutenant Admiral, from November 1958 he assumed the position of Director of the 'Rivista Marittima' and from July 1960 to June 1963 that of Head of the Historical Office of the Stato Maggiore Marina. An effective writer, he published numerous volumes of naval history and commemorative articles on World War II. He died in Naples on 12 December 1968.

Other decorations:

Silver Medal for Military Valour (Central Mediterranean, March 1942 - January 1943);

Bronze Medal for Military Valour (Aegean, May 1941);

Bronze Medal for Military Valour (Central Mediterranean, June 1942);

Bronze Medal for Military Valour (Mediterranean Oriented, August 1942).

Ener BETTICA Lieutenant Commander

Gold Medal for Military Valour in Memory

A superior officer of high fighting virtues, he insisted on embarking on torpedo boats despite the fact that, due to his specific and ingenious technical skills, he was destined to keep a land destination.
Having obtained the command of a destroyer, during a fierce night battle against an adversary formation of cruisers and destroyers, with fearless spirit he twice launched himself to attack the enemy units and, heedless of the violent reaction, with cold daring and serene skill, he succeeded in hitting his torpedoes, from the tightest of distances, with sure destructive effect on one of the adversary ships. He severely hit his unit in several parts, finding himself in the heart of the enemy formation, and having exhausted the torpedoes, he continued for more than half an hour of cannon combat to the extreme limit of every possibility. After providing for the safety of the crew, he sank with the ship under his command, immolating his life always and all proudly dedicated to the Navy, to its progress and to the Homeland.

Sicily Channel, 2 December 1942

He was born in Castagnole Lanze (Asti) on 15 February 190. A pupil at the Livorno Naval Academy from November 1927, on 4 April 1929 he was appointed Ensign and in 1934 he was promoted to Lieutenant of Vessel.

He was in command of the torpedo boat Castelfidardo, then the torpedo boat Prestinari, the torpedo boat Circe and finally the torpedo boat Polluce, with which he began his wartime missions in World War II. Promoted to lieutenant commander in September 1940, he was in charge of the Regia Marina's Centre for Studies and Experiences in Optical Services in Pula from 28 October 1940 to 5 November 1942, and commanded the destroyer Folgore, with which he took part in the mission to escort a convoy loaded with war materials to Bizerte.

Attacked during the night of 2nd December by a preponderant British naval force, composed of three cruisers and two destroyers, he boldly moved into the centre of the enemy formation and, heedless of the violent fire, managed to launch torpedoes that hit the adversary. Having severely hit his unit, when the torpedoes were exhausted, he continued the fight with the cannon; as the ship was about to sink, he saved the crew and, refusing to abandon the ship, he sank with it.

Other decorations:

- Bronze Medal for Military Valour (Central Mediterranean, June 1940).

Alfredo ZAMBRINI, Lieutenant

Gold Medal for Military Valour in Memory

The communications officer of a Ct. Squadron who, in a night battle with a preponderant adversary force, launched himself into the attack with an aggressive spirit and fighting tenacity worthy of the best naval traditions, assisted his commanding officer as always, demonstrating remarkable qualities of serenity, courage and disregard for danger.

When the unit was hit, although severely burned, he was above all concerned with re-establishing communication with the rescue vehicles, overcoming the suffering by which he was tormented with steadfastness and virility.

In the hospital, aware of the imminent end, he heroically faced it, demonstrating his confidence in the victory of Italian arms and praising the Homeland to which he enthusiastically gave his young life.

Central Mediterranean, 2 December 1942.

He was born in Florence on 17 April 1918. After graduating from the Orazio Flacco High School in Bari, he entered the Naval Academy in 1936 and was appointed Ensign in 1939. Promoted to second lieutenant in June 1940, when war was declared he boarded the cruiser Pola and, in October, the torpedo boat Partenope. In March 1941, he embarked on the destroyer da Recco, in the position of Course Officer. In the rank of Lieutenant, which he attained in July 1942, he took part in the epic naval battle sustained by the 16th Destroyer Squadron (of which da Recco was the Squadron Leader), on the night of 2 December 1942 off the Sherki Bank. Wounded in the bitter fighting and shipwrecked, he was picked up and hospitalised first on the hospital ship Toscana and then at the Torrebianca hospital in Trapani, where he died on 14 December from the severity of his wounds.

Other decorations:

Military Distinguished Service Cross (Central Mediterranean, August 1941);

Military Cross for Valour (Central Mediterranean, September 1941);

Military Cross for Valour (Central Mediterranean, February 1942).

THE TORPEDOING OF THE BRITISH CRUISER ARGONAUT BY THE ITALIAN SUBMARINE LAZZARO MOCENIGO

After the destruction of the *Aventino* convoy, the Q Force remained quiet in port for a few days, until the night of 13-14 December, when Rear Admiral Harcourt's cruisers *Orion* and *Argonaut and the* squadron destroyers *Eskimo* and *Quality* (which had replaced the sunken *Quentin*) sailed from Bona to attack, on Ultra information, an Italian convoy bound for Bizerte. The convoy .... The British units were unable to track the Italian convoy, and on their return route, as they proceeded, split into two columns, at a speed of 26 knots, they were attacked at dusk on the morning of 14 December by the Italian oceanic submarine *Lazzaro Mocenigo*, commanded by Lieutenant Commander Alberto Longhi.

The submarine, at 05.58 hours, launched a salvo of four torpedoes targeting the cruiser *Argonaut*, commanded by Captain Eric William Langley-Cook. The 5,450-ton *Argonaut* was hit at lat. 37°30'N, long. 08°13'E by two torpedoes, exploded simultaneously at the bow and stern, which was completely obliterated along with the rudder and two of the four propellers. However, she managed to reach the base at Bona, and then moved to Algiers, and then to Gibraltar for temporary dock work.

But for extensive repairs, carried out at the US dockyard in Philadelphia, where she was escorted from Gibraltar by the destroyer *Hero* (Lieutenant Walter Scott), *the Argonaut*, which had lost only three crewmen in the torpedoing, remained out of service until December 1943 when she was attached to the Home Fleet at Scapa Flow.

The series of photographs that follow are eloquent testimony to the damage done to the cruiser:

▲ The submarine *Lazzaro Mocenigo* photographed on the day of its launch in 1937.

▲▼ The *Argonaut*'s evident damage following the torpedoing of the submarine *Lazzaro Mocenigo*.

▲▼ The condition of the stern of the cruiser *Argonaut* at Bona. If one of the two torpedoes from the submarine Mocenigo had struck amidships, and not at the ends, it is to be assumed that the *Argonaut* would have sunk.

▲ The *Argonaut*'s evident damage following the torpedoing of the submarine *Lazzaro Mocenigo.*

▲ The condition of the stern end of the cruiser *Argonaut*; completely obliterated by a torpedo, sailing from Bona to Algiers on 19 December 1942.

▲ Another detail of the stern of the *Argonaut* sailing for Algiers.

▼ The *Argonaut*'s crew in understandable tension over the perilous journey.

BIBLIOGRAPHY

Official documentation can be found in the notes at the bottom of the page

- Bernotti Romeo, *La guerra sui mari*, volume 2° (1941-1943), Livorno, 1948.

- Bernotti Romeo, *Storia della guerra nel Mediterraneo*, Roma, 1960.

- Bertini Marcello, *I sommergibili in Mediterraneo*, Tomo II, *Dal 1° gennaio 1942 all'8 settembre 1943*, Ufficio Storico della Marina Militare, Roma, 1968.

- Bragadin Marcantonio, *Che ha fatto la Marina?*, Milano, 1955.

- Bragadin Marcantonio, *Il dramma della Marina italiana 1940-1945*, Milano, 1968.

- British Admiralty, *Ships of the Royal Navy, statement of losses*, London, 1947.

- British Admiralty, *Submarines*, volume II: *Operations in the Mediterranean* (non in commercio), Volume II, Londra, 1955.

- Cavallero Ugo, *Diario 1940-1943* (completo nel testo ma privo dei numerosissimi documenti allegati che si possono trovare nella copia del Diario di Cavallero custodita allo Stato Maggiore dell'Esercito Ufficio Storico), Cassino, 1984.

- Connell G.G., *Mediterranean maelstrom. HMS Jervis and the 14th Flotilla*, William Kimber, London, 1987.

- Di Bella Francesco Aurelio., *Un aviatore racconta le sue battaglie*, Palermo, 1950.

- Dorling Taprell [Taffrail], *Mediterraneo occidentale 1942-1945* (traduzione dall'inglese (*Western Mediterranean 1942-1945*), Ufficio Storico della Marina Militare, Roma, 1953.

- Fioravanzo Giuseppe, *Le azioni navali in Mediterraneo. Dal 1° aprile 1941 all'8 settembre 1943*, Volume V, Ufficio Storico della Marina Militare, Roma, 1970.

- Greene Jack. – Massignani Alessandro, *Naval war in the Mediterranean 1940-1943*, Londra, 1998.

- Giorgerini Giorgio, *La guerra italiana sul mare. La Marina tra vittoria e sconfitta. 1940-1943*, Milano, 2001.

- Hinsley F.H. – Thomas E.E. – C.F.G. Ransom – Knight R.C., *British Intelligence in the Second World War*, Volume 3, Parte 1, HMSO, London, 1984.

- Historical Section Admiralty, *Submarines*, vol. II, *Operation in the Mediterranean*, London, 1955.

- Macintyre Donald, *La battaglia del Mediterraneo*, Firenze, 1965.

- Mattesini Francesco – Santoni A., *La partecipazione tedesca alla guerra aeronavale nel Mediterraneo (!940-1945),* Roma 1980. Seconda edizione, collana Storia Militare, Parma 2005.

- Mattesini Francesco, *2 dicembre 1942. La distruzione del convoglio "Aventino" e l'imbarazzante errore del Cacciatorpediniere CAMICIA NERA*, nella pagina dell'autore in *academia.edu.*.

- Mattesini Francesco, *Luci e Ombre degli Aerosiluranti italiani e tedeschi nel Mediterraneo Agosto 1940 – Settembre 1943*; RiStampa Edizioni, Rieti, 2019.

- Playfair I.S.O. e altri, *The Mediterranean and Middle East*, Volume IV, HMSO, Londra, 1960.

- Roskill Stephen Wentworth, *The War at Sea*, Vol. III, Parte I, *The offensive*, Londra, HMSO, 1960.

- Santoni Alberto, *Il vero traditore, Il ruolo documentato di Ultra nella guerra del Mediterraneo*, Milano, 1981.

- Shores Christopher, Massimello Giovanni e Guest Russell, *History of the Mediterranean Air War 1940-1945,* Volune IV, Grub Street, London, 2018.

- Stato Maggiore dell'Esercito Ufficio Storico, *Verbali delle Riunioni tenute dal Capo*

- *di SM Generale*, Volume III, *(1° gennaio – 31 dicembre 1942*), a cura di A. Bigiani, F. Frattolillo e Silvio Maccarelli, Roma, 1985.

- Unia Carlo, *Storia degli aerosiluranti italiani*, Roma, 1974.

TITOLI GIÀ PUBBLICATI - TITLES ALREADY PUBLISHING

BOOKS TO COLLECT

Printed in Great Britain
by Amazon

32244441R00057